Stuff the Turkey

How to survive Christmas with your family

by Steve Caplin and Simon Rose

First published in Great Britain by Simon & Schuster UK Ltd, 2006
A CBS COMPANY

3 5 7 9 10 8 6 4

Simon & Schuster UK Ltd
Africa House
64–78 Kingsway
London WC2B 6AH

www.simonsays.co.uk

Simon & Schuster Australia
Sydney

A CIP catalogue record for this book is available from the British Library.
ISBN–13: 978-0-7432-9514-7
ISBN–10: 0-7432-9514-5

Typeset by Steve Caplin
Printed and bound in Great Britain by The Bath Press, Bath

Contents

With thanks to all those who offered their expertise, in particular:
John Kane, all the Gallimores, Caroline Ashton, Simon Richards, Bill Reiss,
Mireia Mangual, Naoko Mori, Andy Park, Catherine Pease, Charles Clarke,
Cliff Allen of the Grape Street Wine Bar, London (an exceedingly good wine bar),
Rosie Harkin, Gray Watson, Penny Harris, Martin Ball, Mary Berry,
James Caplin, Chris Carr, Pat Graham, Carey Newman, Fiona Tracey,
Anne-Marie Venters, Andrew Corrick, Angela Herlihy, Dawn Bates,
Julian White of the Confrerie du Sabre d'Or and the Bishop of Norwich

... and, of course, our families, for letting us try out so much of this stuff on them.

1 The nights before Christmas

THE KEY TO A SUCCESSFUL CHRISTMAS is planning. That, or hiding on a desert island for a fortnight. If you leave everything until the night before, you may find that your day won't go quite as smoothly as you'd hoped.

Some of the more complex recipes, such as Christmas pudding and mince pies, need to be prepared weeks if not months ahead. Even the least culinary of hosts should ensure they have the essentials in stock before the shops run out of them; it's no good waiting until Christmas morning to find out that your only jar of cranberry sauce has grown an interesting new variety of penicillin since last year.

Seasoned parents will know that you can never have too many batteries, that you need twice as much wrapping paper as you expect, and that receipts really do need to be kept in a safe place rather than wadded up and stuffed into coat pockets.

To avoid falling into one of the dozens of traps that lie in waiting for the unready party giver, we've compiled some of the more useful preparatory tips to ensure your Christmas crackers go with a bang, and not a whimper.

Christmas presents

Whichever fool said it's the thought behind gifts that counts wasn't talking through his mouth. Get the important presents wrong and your Christmas could be frosty, whatever the weather outside.

Present buying: male and female techniques

Women tend to start thinking of Christmas presents shortly after Easter. They'll make copious notes of what to give to whom, where to get it, and what size it should be. If they're buying clothes, they'll have an encyclopaedic knowledge of the recipient's current wardrobe and tastes, and will buy tastefully matching accessories in exactly the right colours. Typically, women will have finished their Christmas shopping by early October.

Men take a different approach, largely due to their ability to filter out the onset of Christmas completely until they've sat through at least three 'Christmas Specials' on television. Advertisements for toys, hair straighteners, two-for-one offers at Boots and perfumes will glide past them unnoticed.

Then, on Christmas Eve, they'll finally get their act together and rush down to the local high street. Snapping up all the glittery items that catch their attention, they'll wait until they get back home with their bags of spoils before deciding what to give to whom. The only people they'll have in mind while actually *buying* the items is their wives or partners, for whom they'll purchase a striking variety of entirely inappropriate lingerie in mismatched colours, and in completely the wrong size.

We're not saying that the female approach is necessarily better. But it does avoid queuing at the returns counter the following week – only to find yourself back where you started, because you've still got to get them presents.

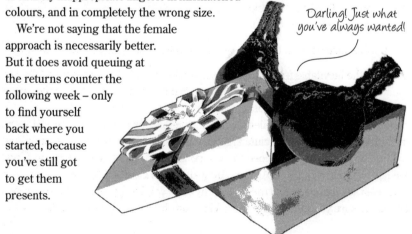

Darling! Just what you've always wanted!

Christmas stockings

There's one very good reason to buy Christmas stockings for children: leave them at the end of their beds on Christmas Eve filled with enough small toys, activity books, sweets and other trinkets, and you'll be sure of an extra couple of hours' sleep the following day while your kids (who will have been awake since 5am) merrily unwrap, compare, play with and then trash the contents.

Forget about taste or price. Plunder the local Pound Shop – this is the one day when it doesn't matter if the junk you buy there only lasts a couple of hours.

The stockings themselves can be bought in a variety of purpose-designed styles. Far better, however, to use the red fishnet stockings sold as novelty items in newsagents and novelty shops: they're cheaper, they last longer, and they seem to be infinitely expandable.

Buying presents for children

Whether it's a remote-controlled car, this year's must-have movie tie-in action figure, or the latest hand-held electronic gizmo, there are three cardinal rules every parent needs to be aware of:

1. Whatever it is, it is likely to need batteries.

2. It will be fixed to its packaging with an astonishing assortment of screws, cable ties, wire twists and tape.

3. If it has instructions, they will be incomprehensible to the average child.

To avoid the inevitable frustration, screaming fits and disappointment that follows the inability to play with a toy *immediately* it is unwrapped, the experienced parent will take all possible precautions.

Batteries should be stockpiled well in advance, in a variety of sizes. As well as the standard AAs, you'll need a clutch of those big fat D batteries for toys that contain motors. Some of them will need the C type instead, and any remote controls will almost certainly require AAAs. Buy them all, just in case.

Loosen any fixings so that they can easily be undone by hand, insert the batteries and make sure you understand the instructions before wrapping anything.

Christmas presents: online and mail order

With gift catalogues dropping through our letterboxes almost daily in the run-up to Christmas, buying presents has never been easier.

When buying from catalogues, aim to get your orders in by the end of November at the latest. The week before Christmas is not the ideal time to be stuck at home waiting for the postie to deliver that one special item.

If your child desperately wants the latest games console, it's no good ordering the cheapest one on the web and then forgetting about it. Online retailers usually run out of the best items first. Unless you get a confirmation that the item has been dispatched within a couple of days, check with them that they actually have it in stock.

Even the mighty Amazon can sometimes sell out and fail to deliver the goods as quickly as you want; make sure you allow enough time to source the items elsewhere if your initial purchase falls through.

Online shopping may be quicker, but if you're pressed for time, it doesn't give you the same comfort as taking a purchase away from a shop in your arms.

I really wanted a girl for Christmas

Remember that many stores now sell online too, often with quick delivery and an indication of what's in stock or not. Shopping in person at Argos may be an experience that Hercules would have balked at, but buying from their website is a pleasure.

When your item does arrive, check to make sure you've been sent exactly what you ordered. However sophisticated the website or catalogue, your order is packed by people and people sometimes make mistakes. If your son has his heart set on an X-Box, he may not be impressed if he ends up with a Cabbage Patch doll instead.

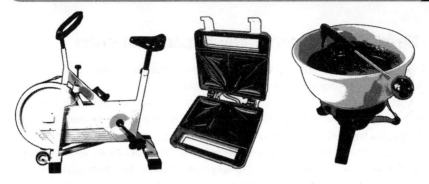

The wrong sort of Christmas present

When it comes to choosing gifts, bear in mind a recent survey carried out for *Pricerunner.co.uk* on household appliances. The least wanted item of all – even when people bought it for themselves – was a fondue set, followed closely by ice-cream makers, keep-fit videos, foot spas, back massagers, toasted sandwich makers and exercise bikes.

The most appreciated new gadget of all was a digital radio.

The battery problem

Even if you're sensible enough to stock up with batteries for your kids' new toys, a little more forethought can save you money. For a start, never buy cheap batteries from the market, even if they are copper and black Duracell lookalikes. In our experience if they're still going by the time Christmas lunch has finished, you'll be lucky.

That doesn't mean batteries have to cost a fortune. We went shopping for some toys for ourselves on the web. Soon our list for Santa included a chunky remote-controlled truck (12 AAs), a voice transformer (9v), a fart machine (4 AAAs) and a man-sized torch (3 Ds). To buy two sets of top name batteries for these at our local convenience store, we would have to shell out £46.28.

Exactly the same batteries could be bought online for £12.78 plus £2.99 postage. Buy in larger quantities and each battery is even cheaper, with the postage free.

If you can't stand having all those batteries then you could always buy a battery charger and some rechargeables, bearing in mind that these are second only to ballpoint pens in their tendency to go missing when you need them.

Make your own Christmas cards

Commercially available Christmas cards – the ones you buy in the shops – are just one way of keeping in touch with your friends and relatives. There's an endless variety on offer – and providing you like snow, robins, angels and Three Wise Men cartoons, you're sure to find one that matches your taste.

If you want something more personal, though, it may be a good idea to design your own card. It needn't be a chore, as long as you think about it before it's too late; and the hand-crafted nature of the cards you send will mean that friends are far more likely to actually *read* them, rather than just stacking them on the mantlepiece with all the others.

The personal touch

Photographs of yourself and your family on cards always go down well – especially if they're shots of you all lying on the beach in the summer, wearing Santa hats.

If you have basic page layout software on your computer and a digital camera, you can incorporate the pictures along with the text; otherwise, get a number of copies printed out and glue them onto the front of your cards.

Hand-made cards

A great solution if you don't have too many cards to send, and you have plenty of time on your hands (or plenty of children to help you).

Start with a simple black and white design, which can be reproduced in small quantities on a laser printer or photocopier; add glitter, pieces of tinsel and those gift bows that come with wrapping paper.

We have a friend who used to design the most intricate cards, colour them in, and then cut each one into a jigsaw puzzle before bagging them up and posting them. Everyone who received one assembled the puzzle!

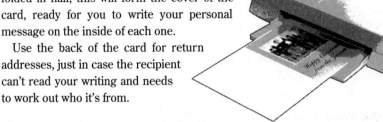

Cards from your inkjet printer

This is a great way of reproducing cards if you're only sending a smallish number. Design your cards using photographs and whatever text you want to fit on half a sheet of A4 paper; when printed and folded in half, this will form the cover of the card, ready for you to write your personal message on the inside of each one.

Use the back of the card for return addresses, just in case the recipient can't read your writing and needs to work out who it's from.

Printed cards

Although it may seem expensive to go to the trouble of getting your cards produced by a professional printer, if you're sending more than about 60 it can still be worth it – and, unlike sending cards from an inkjet printer, they'll be good quality and printed on decent, thick card stock.

Many printers will accept your work online, as long as it's supplied in the right format – either a high resolution JPEG image (which can include text), or a PDF file. If you don't know what either of these are, or how to create them on your computer, then this might not be the best option for you.

The best card printer we've found isn't in the UK but, curiously, in Italy. Their website is *www.pixart.it/uk*, and 100 cards costs around £58 including delivery. Not only are they far cheaper than any UK printer we know of, they're also much quicker – cards are usually delivered within two days of being ordered. Be aware, though, that they do get very busy around Christmas – so if you're planning on using them, sooner rather than later is the best approach.

Just in time?

The Post Office will guarantee (so they say – believe them at your peril) to deliver any cards posted up to a closing date of 19th December for first-class letters and 16th December for second-class (these dates may well change).

But if you're sending cards to business associates, remember that they'll be likely to knock off for Christmas a couple of days early, and the first thing they'll do when they return in January is tip the whole lot into the bin. So if you want them to read the cards, make sure they get there at least a week earlier!

Christmas card etiquette

The way to ward off last-minute Christmas card panic is to think ahead, however much it's out of character. Keep a list of people to send cards to, possibly split into priorities such as 'musts', 'probably shoulds' and 'would be nice tos'. Ideally, store it on a computer, giving the file a name so obvious you can find it the following Christmas.

As you receive cards add the names of those you'd forgotten. Don't forget to add to the list any bosses or contacts you feel the need to crawl to. You might not want to kiss their arse under the mistletoe, but you can do it with a card. Do it early, though. You don't want it to arrive just before Christmas when they're ripping open another 75 they've just received.

It's also worth making a note of who you've sent cards to. One card may be gratefully received. Two, and you obviously don't care enough about the recipient to remember this is the second card. Three, and you're clearly getting a work experience person in your office to send them out.

When you take your cards down after Christmas, check those you have received against your list. If this is the second year you've sent a card to somebody who hasn't returned the favour, cross them off; they've either died, moved or grown tired of getting cards addressed to 'Rita and Jim' when Jim left Rita four years ago to live with his secretary as you would know if you ever did anything more about keeping in touch than sending Christmas cards hastily scribbled in green ink in the wrong-sized envelopes.

Much as you might loathe those people who start organising Christmas around the time the lawn needs its first cut, if you want to send cards to friends or family overseas you must get them done by November or early December at the latest. A reminder to this effect should be the first thing you scribble on that glossy new calendar with pastoral scenes of English villages that Auntie Maureen gave you. You *did* remember to send a card to Auntie Maureen, didn't you?

2 Bottoms up

IT MUST BE POSSIBLE to have a teetotal Christmas, but we've certainly never managed it. The holidays are usually a time where we not only imbibe far too much but also drink all manner of bizarre concoctions that we'd never dream of pouring down our throats at any other time of the year.

Naturally port and champagne will make an appearance so we've got all the dope on these noble drinks. No more need you feel the slightest social embarrassment when someone asks you to pass the port. And if you want to open a bottle of champagne with a sword, like a hussar of old, you can truly make it a Christmas to remember.

Christmas wouldn't be Christmas without the intoxicating smell of mulled wine, so we've included our favourite recipe. For those staying off the booze, we've also included a non-alcoholic hot punch that still packs a kick.

We've recommendations on how to drink without waking up the following morning feeling like death. But if you do get a hangover, we've a wide range of suggestions on how to deal with it.

Toasts

Clinking glasses together to make a toast seems a jolly friendly thing to do. But its origins are rather darker. The Greeks raised glasses and drank from the same barrel simultaneously to prove that the brew hadn't been poisoned. The melodious Scandinavian toast of 'skål' derives from the phrase 'may you drink from the skull of your enemy', as the Vikings did to unwind at the end of a hard day's conquering, pillaging and raping. As for clinking glasses, that was to ward off evil spirits who were said to be repelled by anything that sounded like bells.

'Toast' was originally just that. The Romans reckoned dropping a bit of burnt bread in wine would improve the taste and absorb the impurities. This belief clung on for a long time. In *The Merry Wives of Windsor*, Falstaff orders wine, saying "Go fetch me a quart of sack; put a toast in't." By then, such toast would be spiced or sweetened.

From time to time, toasting was even banned as it was felt to lead to licentiousness and other wickedness. As if…

Some toasts we like

To friendship on a dark road

Sweethearts and wives – may they never meet (Royal Navy)

May you be in heaven half an hour before the devil knows you're dead (Irish toast)

Here's looking at you, kid (Humphrey Bogart)

May you live as long as you want to and may you want to as long as you live

Here's mud in your eye (John Wayne)

Over the teeth, behind the gums, look out stomach, here she comes (Spike Jones)

May you live all the years of your life (Jonathan Swift)

I drink to your charm, your beauty and your brains – which gives you a rough idea how hard up I am for a drink (Groucho Marx)

May the people who dance on your grave get cramps in their legs (A Yiddish toast)

Here's to us all. God bless us everyone (Tiny Tim in *A Christmas Carol*)

Champagne to real friends, and real pain to sham friends

Toasts around the world

Country/language	Suitable drink	Toast
Bali	Arak	Selemat
Brazil	Cachaca	Saude
China	Rice wine	Gan bei
Czech Republic	Becherovka	Na zdravi
England	Tea	Cheers
Esperanto	Vinon	Je via sano
Finland	Cloudberry wine	Kippis
France	Cognac	A votre santé/A le votre
Germany	Schnapps	Prosit
Greece	Ouzo	Yasou
Hungary	Tokay	Egészségedre
Ireland	Guinness	Sláinte
Israel	Sabra	L'chaim
Italy	Chianti	Salute, Cin cin
Japan	Sake	Kanpai
Korea	Yakju	Gun bai
Latin	Honeyed wine	Salutem
Malaysia	Tiger beer	Yam seng
Netherlands	Jenever	Prohst
Norway	Aquavit	Skål
Philippines	San Miguel beer	Mubuhay
Poland	Vodka	Na zdrowie
Portugal	Port	Saúde
Romania	Tuicã	Noroc
Russia	Vodka	Za vashe zdorovye
Saudia Arabia	Water	Hanian
Scotland	Scotch	Slainte mhoiz
Singapore	Gin sling	Yam seng
Spain	Cava	Salud
Sweden	Schnapps	Skål
Thailand	Mekhong whisky	Chook dee
Turkey	Raki	Serefinize
Wales	Leek wine	Hwyll/Lechyd da
Yugoslavia	Slivovitz	Ziveli

Mulling it over

Your very
good elf!

The tradition of serving hot, alcoholic, spicy drinks goes back centuries and is one we're only too happy to help perpetuate. Mulled wine, in particular, helps get any party off to a flying start. It isn't just the warm glow as it goes down, but the sumptuous aroma that permeates the whole room.

Here's our favourite mulled wine recipe which always seems to go down a treat. We can't recall a single occasion on which there has been any left over. In fact after drinking this, we can't recall very much at all.

INGREDIENTS: MULLED WINE

2 bottles of red wine	1 tbsp mixed spice
½ pt orange juice	1 tsp grated nutmeg
oranges and lemons	75g brown sugar
2 cinnamon sticks	¼ bottle of brandy (optional)

Pour the wine into a large saucepan. Don't go for the very cheapest wines but inexpensive is fine, as long as it's fruity. You do *not* want to waste the best bottles in your wine rack. Start warming the wine up gently as you add the orange juice, squeezing in some freshly squeezed orange juice as well. Add some orange and lemon rind. Throw in a couple of cinnamon sticks, a tablespoon of mixed spice, a grated nutmeg (or a teaspoon or so from a tub) and brown sugar to taste. Start with 75g or so and add more later if needed.

Whatever you do, don't let it boil – you will simply be getting rid of the alcohol! If you wish, heat up some brandy in a pan, or in a ladle immersed in the mulled wine. Set fire to the brandy in the ladle and lower it, flaming, into the wine. Slice up some oranges and lemons and float them on top.

Although modern glasses are much less prone to shattering than years ago, you might still want to put a teaspoon into each glass as you pour. If you don't mind how they look, you can always use polystyrene cups. Just in case a glass does shatter (and it never has in our three decades of making the stuff), pour it out at a distance from the rest of the mulled wine. If you've a ladle with a spout, you can pour directly into the glasses, otherwise transfer the hot wine to a jug first and pour from that. Lovely though mulled wine is, the whole business can be pretty messy, increasingly so as the party wears on, so do all the transferring of the mulled wine somewhere that's easy to clean up.

As more people arrive, simply add more wine, spices, orange juice and sugar to the pot. The proportions don't need to be exact. Just keep tasting from time to time to keep things on track. That's certainly what Simon does! He confesses that he no longer bothers with the orange and lemon rind or even the brandy as it's just too fiddly and he's usually had to spend two hours chasing around for anywhere that hasn't run out of cinnamon sticks.

Kane's konkoction

If you want to provide a non-alcoholic hot drink that still has a kick, our friend John Kane has devised a neat one. The use of Tabasco occasionally convinces people at his parties to behave as if they're drunk, even though they haven't imbibed any alcohol at all.

INGREDIENTS

2 litres Diet Coke	$\frac{1}{2}$ tsp mace
2 litres strong Earl Grey tea	$\frac{1}{2}$ tsp ginger
2 litres orange juice	1 tsp Tabasco
$\frac{1}{2}$ tsp cinnamon	1 orange
$\frac{1}{2}$ tsp nutmeg	24 cloves

Mix the Coke, the tea and the orange juice together. To this add cinnamon, nutmeg, mace, ginger and Tabasco sauce to taste, though half a teaspoon of all except the Tabasco (a teaspoon) is a rough guide.

Slice an orange into four pieces and embed the skin of each with half a dozen cloves and float them in the pan, clove-side down. Boil for three minutes, then reduce to a simmer.

As John Kane says, it may sound disgusting – but try it, it goes down a treat.

Red Bullet

This fantastic cold punch will get your party going with a heck of a swing. It achieves exactly the same effect as champagne cocktails but is considerably cheaper. Simon was given the recipe many years ago by Ian Howie, the founder of Merrydown Wine, who had learnt to make alcohol using currants in Red Cross Parcels while a POW in a World War Two Italian camp.

INGREDIENTS

Merrydown vintage dry cider
Gin or vodka
Crème de Cassis (or Ribena!)

For every five measures of Merrydown vintage dry cider (or medium if you want it sweeter), add one measure of gin (or vodka) and two measures of Crème de Cassis. Mix together and serve with ice. If you're serving this drink in summer, chill everything first.

The recipe given out by Merrydown Wine these days is a little different (for every five litre bottles of cider, two 70cl bottles of gin and half a 70cl bottle of Crème de Cassis.) This may simply be because the company no longer produces English country wines, but as you can get Crème de Cassis in some supermarkets we're sticking with the original tried and tested recipe.

The Managing Director of Merrydown Wine has confided in us that after making a first batch of Red Bullet with Crème de Cassis he tends to substitute Ribena – and nobody seems to notice the difference.

Whichever version you go with, serve it in wine glasses rather than tumblers or beer glasses unless you want to risk your entire party doing a conga down the street. As the company is at pains to point out, the current Red Bullet recipe is twice the strength of Smirnoff Ice or a Bacardi Breezer.

Pink Shampoo

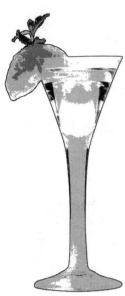

Children like to join in the festive fun, but these days plying them with alcoholic drinks is frowned upon (unless you live in France, where it's considered positively civilised). Here's a safe version of Pink Champagne that's easy to make, looks good, and will help them to feel that they're part of the proceedings (and with no side effects).

INGREDIENTS

200ml of pineapple juice   *100ml of orange juice*
300ml of water   *2 litres of lemonade*
400ml of cranberry juice

Mix all the ingredients together, except the lemonade. This should be added immediately before serving to prevent it going flat. Add a slice of fruit to make it look more exotic, and serve in a tall glass.

Bull in a China Shop

Some party drinks just get you in the right mood for falling asleep. This one has the advantage of not only making you merry, but keeping you partying late into the night – a good one to serve on New Year's Eve, for example.

The original recipe calls for champagne, but frankly that's a waste. We find that Cava, the sparkling wine, works just as well – you can't tell the difference in this mixture, and it's an awful lot easier on the pocket.

INGREDIENTS: BULL IN A CHINA SHOP

1 bottle of Cava
4 cans of Red Bull
1/2 bottle of vodka

Mix everything together. If you want to faff about adding crushed ice and sprigs of holly that's up to you. Frankly, after a couple of glasses you're doing well if you can even find the freezer.

Champagne cocktails

Although it tastes wonderful straight, there's an immense amount you can do with Champagne or indeed any of the other sparkling wines from around the world that are disqualified from calling themselves Champagne.

The most common Champagne cocktail is Buck's Fizz, known elsewhere as Mimosa. A mix of orange juice and Champagne, it was invented in 1921 by a barman at Bucks Club in London. The original also had grenadine; a little orange curaçao is sometimes added these days.

INGREDIENTS

Sugar cube   *Champagne*
Dash of Angostura Bitters
Brandy

To make a proper Champagne cocktail, place a sugar cube (or a teaspoon of sugar) in the bottom of a flute glass and shake a dash of Angostura bitters over it. Pour in brandy until the sugar is covered, and top up the glass with Champagne. Wait for the noise level to rise, and serve to applause.

We prefer using peach schnapps instead of brandy, made in exactly the same way. As it's tricky telling what fizz is used, you may as well use something cheaper than Champagne. A straight mix of Champagne and peach juice (like you'd make Buck's Fizz) is known as a Bellini.

Our friend Cliff, who runs an exceedingly good wine bar, recommends cranberry juice mixed with Champagne. Called a Poinsettia, this is excellent either as an aperitif or with desserts. Kir Royale, a little Créme de Cassis (redcurrant liqueur) topped up with Champagne, is pretty well known but Cliff also recommends using Crème de Mures (blackberries).

Bismarck was said to be very fond of Black Velvet, which mixes Champagne with Guinness (or indeed any stout) in equal proportions, the wine being floated on the stout. Other Champagne mixes are with blueberry schnapps (which has the ungainly name Blow Blue Bubbles), tawny port (Nelson's Blood) and Crème de Framboise (Kir Imperial).

Egg Nog

Any American movie or TV show set at Christmas features Egg Nog, a frothy concoction that was once common in Britain. From the Middle Ages on, hot milk drinks and punches were thought to be good for the health, and often had spices and alcohol added, and later sometimes eggs to thicken them. Known as *possets*, they were served in taverns in a carved wooden pot known as a *noggin*.

In the early 19th century, Pierce Egan's chronicles of the delinquent behaviour of two Regency toffs, *Life in London, or The Day and Night Scenes of Jerry Hawthorn Esq. and his Elegant Friend Corinthian Tom* popularised their tipple, known as *Tom & Jerry*. The phrase became synonymous with pubs and bad behaviour, and was later adopted for the famous cartoon duo.

There are umpteen versions of Egg Nog but this should give you a fairly good idea of what it tastes like. Most people serve it cold – usually in punch glasses – but others swear it tastes better hot. Others swear that Egg Nog is the most disgusting drink there is.

Paranoia about eggs being what it is, you must make up your own mind whether to use raw eggs; they should certainly be as fresh as possible. This is the booziest version we've found and should serve eight. Other recipes use different spirits, such as Kalhua, dark rum, bourbon and brandy, though not usually all at once.

INGREDIENTS

4 eggs	300ml whisky
100g sugar	200ml double or whipping cream
100ml white rum	ground nutmeg to sprinkle
300ml milk	

Separate out the eggs. Beat the yolks with half of the sugar then put the mixture aside. Beat the egg whites until stiff, and add the remaining half of the sugar. Pour the yolks into the egg whites gently, mixing slowly to preserve the fluffiness.

Slowly pour in the white rum, then the milk, then the whisky followed by half of the cream. Whip the rest of the cream and fold it into the mixture very carefully.

Ladle the Egg Nog into cups – trying to get foam and liquid into each cup – and serve at room temperature with a sprinkling of nutmeg. We've been told that if there's any Egg Nog left over, it makes for an interesting variant on French toast. Soak slices of bread thoroughly in the Egg Nog then fry till browned.

THANKS TO CYRIL K COLLINS

Champagne facts and figures

Bubbly, Fizz, Shampoo – whatever you call it, Champagne may be available all year round, but it's only on New Year's Eve that many of us think to buy the stuff. Here are some tips on how to keep it, how to open it, and how it came into being in the first place.

Keep it sparkling

People often swear that dangling a silver spoon in the neck of a Champagne bottle will keep the fizz going. We confess that we have never tested this. For some reason, we can't recall keeping an opened bottle of Champagne overnight.

A few questions in the right corner, however, proved that this solution is nothing more than an old wives' tale – although probably one told by particularly well-off old wives.

A team of researchers at Stanford University actually studied this problem. They found, to their surprise, that the least successful method of preserving opened Champagne is to restopper the wine. Dangling a spoon in the neck worked better than that (though premium Champagne bottles have *very* thin necks so you can't get the spoon in, darling!). The most effective solution was simply leaving the Champagne open.

What seems to happen is that the bubbles in Champagne (or any other sparkling wine produced by a similar method) are carbon dioxide. It's a heavy gas so, after you pop the cork and pour a glass or two, the bubbles settle on top of the wine, sealing it and preventing it from oxidising. Put the bottle back in the fridge and the bubbles under the surface will stay safely in liquid form for 24 hours or so.

This has since been confirmed by the *Comité Interprofessionnel des Vins de Champagne*, who say that a spoon inserted into the neck, whether silver or not, has no effect on the Champagne's *éventage* or "loss of gas".

Champagne sizes

Not sure what size bottle to buy? Let this handy reference chart be your guide. Sizes compared to a standard bottle are shown, along with the rather bizarre biblical names that they've acquired.

Do you feel lucky, punk?

1 — Bottle
2 — Magnum
4 — Jeroboam
6 — Rehoboam
8 — Methuselah
12 — Salmanazar
16 — Balthazar
20 — Nebuchadnezzar
24 — Melchior

Jeroboam I was a king of northern Israel, who died in 912 BC.
Rehoboam was the son of Solomon, who died in 922 BC.
Methuselah was the oldest man in the Bible, who supposedly lived for 969 years.
Salmanazar is derived from Salma, a measure of liquid used in Italy.
Balthazar was one of the Three Wise Men.
Nebuchadnezzar was King of Babylon from 605 to 562 BC.
Melchior was supposedly another of the Three Wise Men.

There are also three further sizes of bottle – Solomon (33.3 bottles), Primat (36 bottles) and the ludicrously massive Melchizedek (40 bottles), but modesty forbids us from depicting them here.

How to open Champagne

Unless you've just won the Silverstone Grand Prix or the Ashes, shaking a bottle of Champagne and spraying the contents over everyone is just not on. Apart from the obvious vulgarity of such an action, it's a waste of what is – for most of us – a fairly expensive and special drink.

Instead, chill the Champagne in the fridge for three or four hours, or in a bucket – in a mixture of ice and water – for half an hour. Remove the foil so you can get to the twisted wire at the bottom of the cork. If the bottle is slippery, wipe it down or wrap a napkin around it and, keeping your hand on the cork, untwist the loop keeping the wire cage in place over the cork.

Open out the cage and remove it along with any remaining foil. Holding the Champagne bottle around stomach level at a 45° angle, ensure that it isn't pointing towards any priceless Ming vases or relatives you're particularly fond of. The Champagne is, after

You don't need a proper ice bucket, but it looks so much better than the plastic variety

all, under 80 pounds per square inch of pressure (two or three times the pressure in your car tyres). Holding the cork firmly with one hand, *twist the bottle* with the other. Pushing the cork with your thumbs is wrong; there's a risk it might break. If you think some twit might have shaken the Champagne as a lark, you can always put a tea towel over the cork. This is also a good precaution if you're worried it's not cold enough, as the pressure increases with temperature.

You aren't aiming for a loud pop. Particularly pompous wine snobs will tell you that "the ear's gain is the palate's loss", and they're right. Shake the fizz to get that satisfying noise and you not only risk losing Champagne but also many of the bubbles that give it its character.

Whatever you do, don't be tempted to put Champagne in the freezer to chill it quickly. Not only does it upset the taste, but there's also a risk of the bottle exploding if the wine freezes. Although it's okay to leave Champagne in the fridge for a few hours, don't store it there or you'll ruin the flavour.

If a cork does fly out, it does so at 30 miles an hour. It can do serious damage at that speed, particularly as it fits so neatly in an eye socket.

How to serve Champagne

If properly chilled and opened, you shouldn't lose any Champagne as the cork comes out – but it's still common sense to have a glass handy, just in case.

But which glass should you serve it in? The stubby, saucer-shaped coupe was the favourite with the Victorians, despite – or perhaps because – it was said to have been moulded from Marie Antoinette's breast. Oddly, this is one of those supposed 'myths' that may actually be true. The Sèvres porcelain plant certainly did take a cast of the Queen's breast to make four bowls for her model dairy.

However, the coupe isn't ideal for drinking Champagne. It isn't just that these glasses are smaller than the original model. They're very hard to hold without the hand warming the Champagne, while their large surface area results in the effervescence disappearing too quickly. Far better to use long-stemmed flutes, which concentrate the bouquet, retain the bubbles better and, providing you hold the stem, keep the champers colder. Crystal is better than plain glass, both for appearance and quality: more bubbles will form on its rougher texture.

Pour a little into each glass first, letting the foam die down before topping them up. That way you won't be in danger of the Champagne frothing over the top of the glasses. Oh, and remember to keep a glass for yourself.

If serving Champagne to toast in the new year at the end of the evening, don't get carried away and open every bottle in sight: by that stage, many people will only want a sip.

The other one's an elf hazard

The right sort of glass to serve Champagne

The wrong sort of glass – unless you're a particular fan of Marie Antoinette's boobs

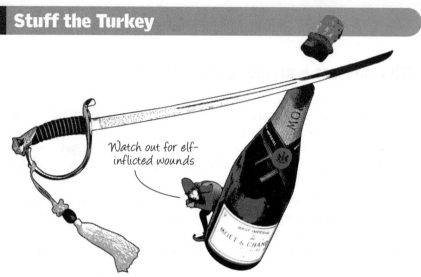

Watch out for elf-inflicted wounds

The military approach to opening Champagne

Legend has it that before battle, French hussars would lop the top off a bottle of Champagne with their sword, quaffing the fizz to give themselves Dutch courage. The practice – *sabrage* – has been a feature of army messes around the world for generations and experts in the art now perform it at posh dinners.

You probably don't have a sword lying around. But that's no reason you should feel left out. If you don't want to opt for a Champagne sabre (which can be bought online) use something solid like a chunky kitchen knife. Not quite as impressive perhaps, even if you attach to the handle the bit of rope that usually holds back the curtains, but it's still pretty amazing if your audience hasn't seen it done before.

Chill your Champagne as normal then remove the foil and the cage. Providing it hasn't been shaken up, the cork should stay in the bottle but be prepared, just in case. Look at the neck and you'll notice a slight seam on either side. Hold the bottle securely in one hand at a 30° angle from horizontal with one of the seams on top. Ensuring nobody's in the line of fire, take your sabre (or kitchen knife). At about a 15° angle away from the bottle, slide it sharply up the neck with your elbow held high, hitting the glass bump below the cork (the annulus) on the seam with the blunt side.

As the glass is cold and you are hitting the bottle at its weakest point, the annulus should shear off neatly with a loud pop, taking the cork with it. A little Champagne will gush out of the neck, removing any possible splinters but not robbing you of too much of the wine.

Champagne – an English invention

It is often claimed that the French monk Dom Perignon – cellar master of the Benedictine Abbey of Hautvillers – invented Champagne around 1695. A little inconveniently for the story, British winemaker Christopher Merret had presented a paper at the Royal Society over 30 years earlier explaining how to make sparkling wine by adding sugar and molasses to make it ferment a second time. Until then, wine that came out of the bottle fizzy was considered a mistake.

At that time, Champagne was a still white wine that sometimes fermented twice accidentally – once before the winter set in and then again with the warmer weather in spring. This caused the bottles to explode, sometimes losing up to a third of their production. It was a dangerous business, and iron masks were worn to prevent glass shards being fired into eyes by the explosions. The French soon became irritated that the English had taken a fancy to sparkling wine and were importing their still Champagne to make it. They wanted to produce it themselves.

Drinking stars? Seeing stars, more likely

It wasn't until the 1690s that the French could manufacture bottles that were strong enough for sparkling wine. Using these, Dom Perignon developed a more consistent grape blend, replacing the oil-soaked cotton used to stopper bottles with corks tied on with string.

When he got it right, he's said to have shouted, "Brothers, brothers, come quickly! I am drinking stars!" It still wasn't until the 1800s that winemakers learnt how to control the pressure inside Champagne bottles and thus bring about the glory days of Champagne.

The Champagne climate is similar to southern England and in the 18th century we produced a great deal of sparkling wine. That from Painshill in Surrey – recently replanted and now producing wine again – was so good that the Duc de Mirepoix, the French ambassador, was annoyed to discover that he had mistaken it for Champagne.

Dom Perignon: among the best, but he wasn't the first

Port: the drink of philosophers

Port, usually made from black grapes in Portugal's *Douro* region, is said to be the 'drink of philosophers' ("I think I'm drunk therefore I am"). You've probably got a bottle tucked away in a cupboard somewhere: now is the time when this prince among drinks should be wheeled out.

Naval fortification

One drawback of war with France in the late 17th century was that the British couldn't drink French wine and had to find it elsewhere. Sailors bringing back Portuguese wine that hadn't finished fermenting added brandy to help preserve it. This fortified the wine and sweetened it. Pretty soon, like the French with Champagne, the Portuguese reckoned that if that was the way the mad English wanted their wine, they'd make it that way.

Stronger than wine (around 20 per cent by volume), port usually comes out at the end of a meal. It is remarkably easy to drink in quantity yet, as a dark drink full of congeners (see page 28), there is also an unfortunate downside.

Decanting the port

Decent ports should be decanted, as there could be sediment in the bottle that you don't want in your drink. The whole business of decanting adds to the pleasure, though you can easily justify it by claiming that it also brings out the bouquet and flavour. If you're serving vintage port, experts recommend leaving it for a few hours in the decanter (young seven-year-olds for 10 hours, 60-year-olds only an hour or two). Ensure your decanter is not only clean and devoid of dust but also free of soapy stuff. Rinse it out with warm and cold water at least once.

Some time beforehand (several hours, if not a couple of days), stand the bottle upright so that the sediment sinks to the bottom. Remove the cork without shaking the bottle, and simply pour it into a decanter, taking care not to let any sediment come out. It's best to use a funnel so you can spot the sediment. If you don't have one, nobody's going to know if you transfer the port to a kitchen jug. Hold the bottle over a candle (or get someone to hold a torch) to illuminate the neck as you pour it out.

The problem with this method is that you don't get all the port out. If it's a really old port, the cork may crumble away as you try to remove it. So filtering it through a piece of untreated cheesecloth or muslin, doubled over, is sensible. This way you can get out every last drop. Filtering the port also removes the necessity for getting it ready in advance and letting the sediment settle.

If you have a baby around, you may have muslin in the house without realising it: that's what those squares for tidying up baby goo are made from. We shouldn't have to tell you to wash it first. There's sediment and then there's *sediment*.

Nylon will do too, apparently. Anybody around the table wearing anything made of nylon? Hang on, there's a party game in the making here.

Pass the bishop, old chap

Port-drinking has an associated etiquette. It is always passed to the left, though this long pre-dates the drink. In Homer's *Iliad*, Hephaistos pours wine to all the gods "from right to left". Many cultures think passing from right to left is lucky: a Tibetan prayer wheel, for instance, is always turned in a clockwise direction.

Nobody should pour their own port. The host first serves the guest to their right, then passes the decanter to their left. That guest pours for the host before passing the decanter left, and so on around the table. It is considered bad form to ask for a glass of the stuff. Indeed, saying "pass the port" marks you out as a bounder, if not an outright cad.

It is always possible after a long meal that the port may get stuck. The guest nearest the decanter should then be asked if they know the Bishop of Norwich. If the guest doesn't understand, it's acceptable to say, "Awfully nice chap, the Bishop, but he never passes the port."

Naturally, we felt we had to ask the real Bishop of Norwich what happens at *his* table. To our delight, he replied, saying he does sometimes serve port: "'Do you know the Bishop of Norwich?' would seem a rather eccentric way of getting the decanter moving again around my own dining table… but we haven't had to employ it too much since I've noticed the decanter is soon empty. Whether this is a commentary on the guests I entertain, I'm not sure!"

What on earth are *we* going to do now that we, too, know the Bishop of Norwich?

Any port in a storm

There are two types of port: those aged in the bottle and those aged in the cask. Ports aged in the wood lose colour and become 'tawny'. They are filtered before being bottled and are ready to drink immediately. The superior bottle-aged ports spend much less time in casks and are bottled without being filtered, maturing in the bottle.

Vintage port is the real stuff, with prices to match. Dark ruby in colour and accounting for just 2 per cent of port production, it's made from the red grapes of one particular – vintage – year. It is aged in barrels for two or three years and then for a great deal longer in the bottle, perhaps as much as 50 years. These are the most expensive ports and can in some cases be drunk decades after they're made. The best of the recent vintages are 2003, 2000*, 1997, 1995, 1994*, 1992, 1991, 1985*, 1983, 1977*, 1970*, 1966 and 1963*, the asterisks indicating the truly outstanding years. Ports younger than 20 years should be put aside to mature.

Tawny port is more golden brown and aged for six years or more in wood. Any age on the label (which may be as much as 40 years) is an average of several vintages. Tawny ports can be drunk or kept but they won't improve with age.

Late-bottled vintage port tries to give some of the taste of vintage port without having to hang around too long. The product of a single vintage, it is aged for four to six years in the barrel, maturing more quickly than vintage port. Smoother and less complex than vintage ports, they're usually filtered and are ready to drink without decanting. These will have the stopper type of cork. If they have wine bottle corks then they are unfiltered, traditional LBV ports which may improve in the bottle and will need to be decanted. Late-bottled non-vintage (LBNV) or vintage character port is similar to LBV but is made from grapes of different years.

The most basic, least expensive sort of port, ruby, uses grapes from several vintages and is fermented in wood (or stainless steel these days) for two or three years. Dark and fruity, ruby – a word which doesn't even appear on many labels – should be drunk fairly quickly.

Crusted port, which develops sediment in the bottle, is made from the grapes of different years and bottled after three years. White port is rarely served but can be delicious. Sweet, it's a lovely dessert wine while the dry stuff makes a great aperitif, straight or with ice.

Stilton: the King of Cheeses

Until it was bypassed by the A1(M), travellers on the Great North Road in Cambridgeshire passed through the village of Stilton, 80 miles north of London. The village is, of course, famous for giving its name to the King of Cheeses.

Oddly, though, the cheese has never been made there. Stilton was a staging post in the 18th century and the landlord of the Bell Inn, Cooper Thornhill, served the gorgeous soft, blue-veined cheese to travellers resting at this first stop on the route north. They spread the word about how good it was, not realising that he bought it from a farmer's wife, Frances Pawlett, near Melton Mowbray. Now it's made in one of six dairies in Derbyshire, Leicestershire and Nottinghamshire.

Although traditionally served with port, Stilton goes beautifully with many wines and, unlike other cheeses, can be frozen for up to three months.

Stilton pâté

Although great as a snack at any time, this pâté is a particularly good way to finish off the Stilton when there seems to be almost as much rind as cheese. Get rid of the rind, and crumble the Stilton in a bowl. Gradually pour in a little port, stirring as you go. Don't use a blender. You're aiming for a sludgy consistency still containing discernible chunks of Stilton.

We're the first to admit that it looks a vile, grey colour but on toast or crackers it tastes absolutely wonderful.

Stuffed avocado with Stilton

A delicious recipe – as long as you aren't watching the calories!

INGREDIENTS

Ripe avocados with large stones	*1 tbsp Double cream or crème fraîche*
1 tbsp Stilton for each avocado	*for each avocado*
Walnut halves (optional)	*Lemon juice*

Heat the oven to 200°C, 400°F, gas mark 6. Halve each avocado, remove the stone and brush the exposed flesh with lemon juice. Mix together Stilton with cream (or crème fraîche) to make the cheese a little smoother. Don't make it too runny, as it will melt in the oven. Spoon the mixture into the centre of the avocados and bake them for 10 minutes or so until the cheese has melted; top with walnut halves.

Hangovers: the day after

Q: What's the best thing for a hangover?
A: Drinking heavily the night before.

What is a hangover, anyway?

The barman who asks, "What's your poison?" knows what he's talking about. Taken in excess, alcohol is converted by your body into *acetaldehyde*, a toxin, causing headaches, nausea and possibly an unfortunate pilgrimage to worship the great white porcelain god.

You pee more, too, which can lead to dehydration and loss of essential salts while *congeners* – another toxin – irritate the stomach. Darker drinks contain more congeners than light. So white wine, gin and vodka – while still getting you as drunk – have a less unfortunate after-effect than red wine, brandy and port. Although champagne is light on the congeners, its bubbles speed up the absorption of alcohol into the bloodstream.

It's thought that headaches are exacerbated by increased urination. The body grabs water from where it can, including the brain, which actually shrinks, tugging at its covering – the *dura* – which is lined with pain-sensitive filaments. So if you remember, drink water in conjunction with the booze.

I keep seeing elves

Personally, we never have hangovers. Instead, we get occasional attacks of *veisalgia*, the synonymous medical term. As almost nobody knows what veisalgia is, we can maintain that our 'illness' isn't self-inflicted and hope for sympathy instead of scorn.

Hangovers around the world

'Hangover', a word invented in America after World War I, seems unduly prosaic compared to the florid descriptions that abound in other languages. Here's how some countries describe that morning-after feeling.

Portugal	*Ressaca*	Undertow (choppiness of the sea)
Italy	*Malessere dopo una sbornia*	Sickness after a piss-up
Slovakia	*Opica*	(To have a) monkey
France	*Gueule de bois*	Mouth of wood
	J'ai mal aux cheveux	My hair is ill
Germany	*Katzenjammer*	Wailing of the cats
Sweden	*Hont i haret*	Pain in the root of your hairs
Poland	*Kociokwik*	The moaning of kittens
Japan	*Futska yoi*	Two days drunk
Norway	*Jeg har tommermen*	I have carpenters in my head

Avoiding hangovers

Scientists seem pretty united in recommending that you get some fatty, high-protein stuff inside you before the boozing begins. A large glass of milk, nuts or cheese scoffed in advance will slow down the absorption of alcohol and lessen any possible hangover.

While drinking, in addition to avoiding booze high in congeners (see left), try not to mix it with carbonated drinks. That just speeds up the pace at which the alcohol gets into the blood. So spritzers aren't such a good idea, after all. Alternating booze with soft drinks or water will also reduce potential hangover problems.

On returning home, many swear by a large glass of water or two to counter dehydration before stumbling noisily up the stairs to Bedfordshire. When you're one over the eight, you're a touch hypoglycaemic, with lowered blood-sugar levels. So something with glucose in, like Ribena, is an even better idea, both before bed and when you get up.

Dealing with hangovers

According to a study carried out by Exeter's Peninsular Medical School and published in the *British Medical Journal*, most available hangover cures provide little relief the morning after. The only things they tested that had any noticeable effect were an extract of gamma linolenic acid from the herb borage, the yeast-based supplement *Morning Fit* and tolfenamic acid, a painkiller prescribed for migraine and generally known as *Clotam*.

I've been a little too elf-indulgent

The most sensible way of avoiding a hangover, they concluded, was to avoid drinking in the first place. Ridiculous. Apart from anything else, other scientists tell us that a modest daily intake of alcohol makes us live longer and less likely to develop Alzheimer's disease. Odd, really, when you think how a large amount in just one evening does tend to lead to temporary memory loss.

The Royal Society of Chemistry reckons that a plate of bread and butter with honey or golden syrup is just the thing for the hangover breakfast. They claim it replenishes the store of potassium, sodium and fructose and speeds up the rate of recovery, relieving the headache, reducing sweating and settling nausea. Drinking fluid high in glucose or sweet tea helps, though coffee – a diuretic – should be avoided. So too should sports drinks if they're fizzy, as they really won't do your stomach any favours.

They found no evidence that the traditional fry-up helps, even though the drop in blood sugar levels does make people crave fatty foods. Eggs *are* good, though, and they also recommend scrambled eggs on wholemeal bread or porridge as

good ways of restoring blood-sugar levels.

If you find yourself with a truly bodacious hangover and feel the need for painkillers, avoid aspirin, which may irritate the stomach.

Vive la différence

There was excitement early in 2006 when a French company announced a miracle hangover cure that speeds up the disappearance of alcohol from the system by a factor of six, as well as helping digestion after a heavy meal. Called *Security Feel Better* (it probably sounds better in French), it's made from water, plant extracts, artichoke, fructose, Yunnan tea, ascorbic acid, sodium benzoate and pear flavouring. Its manufacturers claim that a man who drank whisky, a whole bottle of wine and then a liqueur gave a reading of 187mg blood alcohol before taking *Security Feel Better*, but 80mg only 40 minutes later – concidentally, the legal British limit for driving.

Presumably worried about hordes of Brits nipping across the Channel to pick up bottles of the stuff along with their cheap booze, the French abruptly banned it. It's now unbanned and available online – buy it before it's banned again.

The Aussie way

Although ostensibly sold as a vitamin supplement, many Australians swear by *Berocca* as a hangover cure. This aims to replace the vitamins and chemicals lost in a heavy drinking session. Apparently delegates to conferences 'Down Under' often find tubes of the stuff waiting for them in the morning.

It can be bought in the UK, although the only claim made for it here is that it "helps you stay sharp".

The whirling pits

If you've really overindulged then, as you lie down, hoping for oblivion and comforting sleep, you may instead find yourself apparently tumbling through space, head over heels. The whirling pits is not pleasant – though people pay good money for the same experience in a theme park. Although you may swear you'll never touch a drop again, that's little use to you at that particular vertiginous moment.

One way of diminishing the effect of this is to hold onto something solid like a bedside table. Grabbing hold of your sleeping partner for stability is recommended only in exceptional circumstances.

The hair of the dog

Drinkers in many countries believe in the hair of the dog, so called in Britain because the old-fashioned remedy for treating a dog bite was to place some of its fur on the wound. Wounded by booze? Drink some more of the same. In France it's called *rallumant la caudière* (relighting the boiler), while the Danes say *Rejse sig ved det træ, hvor man er faldet*, which means returning to the tree under which you passed out.

In their study of hangovers, the Royal Society of Chemistry debunked the efficacy of the hair of the dog, which merely delays a full recovery. If drinking more alcohol really does make you feel better, it's an indication you might be getting addicted.

Hangover 'cures' we haven't tried

Ever since alcohol was invented, people have been coming up with new ideas for curing hangovers. We can't vouch personally for any of these supposed cures – our local supermarket doesn't yet stock horse brain or sheep's eyes, pickled or otherwise – but if you're really desperate, these may prove to be some use.

- The Ancient Egyptians drank cabbage water.

- Pliny the Elder recommended "two eels suffocated in wine" or rare owl eggs.

- Cato, the Roman senator, believed in eating a bowl of stewed cabbage topped with raw almonds.

- In the Middle Ages, an eel with chopped almonds was the preferred 'cure'.

- In the 19th century, chimney sweeps took warm milk with a teaspoon of soot.

- Puerto Rico: rub the juice of a lemon under your armpits.

- Eastern Europe: drinking brine from a jar of pickled cucumbers to restore salts and other minerals.

- Northern Europe: pickled herring is claimed to be rich in minerals (though the Dutch prefer it raw).

- Mongolia: a glass of tomato juice containing a pickled sheep's eye.

You look a bit off colour to me

- France: onion soup.

- Bucharest: cabbage soup.

- India: Mulligatawny soup (brings out the sweats wonderfully).

- Romania: *ciorbă de burtă* (tripe soup with vegetables).

- China: eating a small amount of horse brain the morning after a night of overindulgence.

- TV chef Keith Floyd, surely an authority on this subject, recommends an electrolyte powder called *Lactade*, which is designed to offset dehydration and replace salts and sugars in… dogs. That's right. A vet mate of his suggested that it was good for hangovers, as well as helping man's best friend get over a potentially fatal form of gastroenteritis. You can try *Dioralyte* instead, intended for humans, if you don't fancy a shiny wet nose.

The Prairie Oyster

This traditional cure was invented in the Jazz Age by Harry MacElhone, the Harry of Harry's Bar in Paris. It must be good, because it not only revived Ernest Hemingway and Scott Fitzgerald but is pretty much what Jeeves prepares for Bertram Wooster in the novels of P G Wodehouse. Jeeves is never wrong.

INGREDIENTS

1 egg yolk
1 tbsp Worcestershire sauce
Salt and pepper

dash of Tabasco
1 tsp malt vinegar

Mix all the ingredients together and drink quickly. You have to drink it quickly because if you take a sip, there's nothing on earth that will persuade you to finish the glass. These days, raw eggs come with their own health warning – so unless you always have a stock of organic, free-range eggs to hand, you may decide this cure is potentially worse than the hangover itself.

Rumpots

The rumpot or *rumtopf* is a German and Austrian tradition that deserves to be more fashionable, particularly as it gives you deliciously boozy fruit and a fruity liqueur in the depths of winter. Make it in the summer, and enjoy it next Christmas!

Rumpots themselves, big ceramic jars with wide lids, can be bought in 3–5 litre sizes though any big, non-metallic jar should be fine. As fresh fruit becomes available each year (it's usually strawberries first), wash and dry a quantity, removing any stems, and put them in a dish. Cover this first batch with an equal weight of castor or white refined granulated sugar. Leave the sugar to soak into the fruit for an hour and then put the whole lot into the rumpot, covering it with an inch or so of rum of at least 40 per cent alcohol by volume. Put the rumpot in a cool, dark place and leave it.

As each new fruit comes into season, add that, using half the weight of sugar from then on. As you add each new fruit to the rumpot, top up the alcohol if necessary. The fruit must stay submerged, so place a saucer on the surface to keep it under. It's best to cover the mouth of the rumpot with clingfilm as well as the lid to cut down evaporation. It requires immense willpower not to dip into the rumpot early but it needs time to ferment and mature and it will be at its best from the holiday season on.

Use ripe but not overripe fruit. It should be fresh, not canned or frozen. The best fruits are strawberries, blackcurrants, raspberries (don't wash raspberries!), plums (cut in half), peaches (cut into pieces), cherries, pears (not the juicy sort), pineapple (in cubes) and grapes. Avoid melon, rhubarb, juicy pears, apples, bananas, citrus fruit and blackberries: they go too soft and squishy. The fruit is delicious with ice cream or yoghurt, or on its own with cream. You can add the liqueur from the rumpot or drink it straight. Yummy.

The Royal Navy knew the preserving power of rum. The body of Admiral Nelson was placed in a large cask of it to preserve him on the trip home after the Battle of Trafalgar. Although it's probably untrue, rumours that the sailors illicitly tapped the barrel to get at the rum led to the naval phrase 'tapping the admiral', meaning illegal drinking. You can use other spirits such as brandy (called a tutti-frutti) or cognac, just so long as it's 40 per cent abv.

I see no ships

3 Christmas traditions

WHAT DOES *Svaty Mikalas* have to do with Good King Wenceslas? Why do Austrian children fear the *Krampus* and French children *Père Fouettard*? You may think Christmas is all holly and mince pies, but there's a wealth of tradition in other countries that will leave you dumbfounded. And you simply won't believe what the Catalonians put in their nativity scenes.

Just in case you're ever abroad at this time of year, we show you how to give seasonal greetings in a range of languages from Icelandic to Urdu. For those who prefer to experience their foreign cultures once they've been fermented, we've included toasts in a variety of languages to match that bizarre array of wines and spirits you've been smuggling through customs for years.

Our own customs also come under the festive microscope. Here you'll find the origin of the Christmas tree, as well as some useful tips for looking after one of your own; discover who sent the first Christmas card, what Queen Victoria had for Christmas lunch, and check your own favourites against our lists of the top Christmas movies and books.

The global origins of Christmas

The 23rd largest lake in the world is Lake Reindeer, in Canada. The 22nd largest is Lake Rudolf, in Kenya.

Father Christmas was introduced to the West in the poem *Twas the Night Before Christmas*, published in the *Troy Sentinel* in 1822.

The poem *Rudolph the Red-Nosed Reindeer* was written in 1939 for a Montgomery Ward Christmas catalogue.

Turkeys originated in Mexico and were brought to Europe in the 16th century.

The name Santa Claus is taken from the Dutch name *Sinterklaas*.

Queen Charlotte of Mecklenburg-Strelitz, wife of George III, introduced the Christmas tree to Britain in the 1760s.

During the mid-winter festival in Siberia, the shaman enters a yurt through the chimney with a sack of fly agaric mushrooms as gifts.

The Russian figure *Ded Moroz* (Grandfather Frost) wears a red coat, fur boots and a long white beard when delivering presents to children.

Christmas Island (pop. 1,500)

During the winter festival of *Saturnalia*, the Romans feasted and exchanged gifts. According to the Julian calendar, the winter solstice fell on December 25th.

A Roman mosaic in Tunisia shows the god Dionysus carrying a tapering fir tree – the first Christmas tree reference.

Saint Nicholas was Bishop of Myra in Lycia (now in Turkey) in the 4th century AD.

Christmas traditions around the world

So you think Christmas is weird in your house? You don't know the half of it. Traditions in other countries are bizarre, exotic, entertaining and sometimes just downright odd.

Here's how Christmas is celebrated in some of the countries you might visit soon.

 Australia It's summer and the end of the school year, but it's still winter on Christmas cards with Santa and snow. Many eschew turkey in favour of plates of prawns. With temperatures as high as 100°F, lunch for many consists of barbies on the beach or in the backyard. On Bondi Beach 'Santa' surfs in. Presumably because there are so few chimneys for him to come down.

Austria The *Krampus* – a horrid devil-like monster – comes to bad children on St Nicholas Eve (5th December). Youths, particularly in the Alps, wear masks and go on riotous *Krampusläufe* to beat badness out of those who deserve it.

Brazil *Papa Noel* ditches his familiar sleigh, and instead arrives from Greenland by helicopter at a soccer stadium in Rio, clad in a silk shirt. And presumably trousers, although that isn't clear.

 Catalonia Nativity scenes in this part of Spain routinely feature a character called *Caganer* (left), tucked away in a corner. And for good reason: the word translates into English as 'The shitter', and depicts a man (sometimes a woman) excreting. The figure has been around since the 18th century: the idea is that he's fertilising the earth, albeit in a rather public fashion. Since the 1940s the original peasant figure has been replaced with nuns, priests, even the Pope – and, more recently, Osama bin Laden.

Chile *Viejito Pascuero* (Old Man Christmas) slips in through open windows with his sack of toys. Open windows? Of course – it's mid summer in Chile.

China As the world's largest manufacturer of Christmas paraphernalia, the Chinese are increasingly getting into the festivities. It has no religious overtones but is simply a way of letting off steam, particularly in big cities, and giving presents, often with Western-style trimmings. Chinese Christians hope for presents from *Dun Che Lao Ren* (Christmas Old Man).

Cyprus December 24th is the 'oracle of love', with a leaf of an olive tree thrown on a fire in order to predict the state of your love life over the following year.

Czech Republic Formerly Bohemia, this is the 10th-century home of King Wenceslas. *Svaty Mikalas* is believed to shin down to earth from heaven on a golden rope. To predict the future, apples are cut in two crossways. If there's a star in the core, the year ahead will be good; a cross and it will be bad. A girl throws a shoe behind her. If the toe points to the door, she's going to get married.

Denmark The Christmas feast is at midnight on Christmas Eve. A single almond is hidden in a rice pudding and whoever finds it will have good luck for the following year. Santa is called *Julemanden*, and his elves are *Juul Nisse*. Children leave out milk or rice pudding for them.

Finland Here they believe Father Christmas lives in Korvatunturi, the northern part of the country above the Arctic Circle. Presents are given on Christmas Eve by someone dressed up as him.

Can I come out now?

France Children put their shoes by the fireplace on Christmas Eve for *Père Noel* to fill them – assuming they haven't been bad. If they have, *Père Fouettard* (Father Spanker) will exact his revenge. French grown-ups often don't exchange presents until New Year's Eve, *la Saint-Sylvestre*, which is an adult celebration.

Germany Presents are usually given on Christmas Eve. Children get theirs from the *Weihnachtsmann* (Christmas Man) or the *Christkind* (Christ Child). Trees often have real candles.

 Gisborne, New Zealand The first city to celebrate Christmas each year. This is more to do with its geographical location than any over-enthusiastic jumping of the gun.

 Great Britain Utterly bizarre. People sit around a table wearing silly paper hats and reading out staggeringly bad jokes. After lunch they turn on the TV and their monarch graciously lulls them to sleep.

 Greece Most ships have an image of St Nicholas on board – he's the patron saint of sailors. Instead of Christmas trees, homes have a sprig of basil in a bowl. This, together with constant fires, is to repel the *Killantzaroi*, mischievous goblin-like spirits who only strike during the 12 days of Christmas. Gifts are exchanged on January 1st, St Basil's Day.

 India Hindus and Muslims celebrate Christmas as a secular holiday, decorating mango and banana trees with ornaments. At least they don't drop pine needles all over the carpet.

Italy Epiphany (January 6th) is the day for gifts, but they are left by *La Befana*, an old woman who was too busy cleaning to help the Wise Men out. She flies around on her broom and goes down chimneys to leave gifts or coal. Families draw lottery tickets to see who gets which present.

 Japan Although Christmas Day isn't a public holiday, Santa Claus, Christmas trees and Western Christmas music are now common. Gift-giving is more romantic, akin to Valentine's Day, while New Year's Day is for family celebrations more like our Christmas.

 Mexico Children attack a cardboard or papier mâché *piñata* hanging by a rope, which contains sweets and gifts. Better than beating up each other, which is what tends to happen here.

 Netherlands Saint Nicholas Day, December 6th, is more important than Christmas. Children leave out shoes the evening before for *Sinterklaas*, who lives in Spain and arrives in mid-November by steamship, covered live on TV. He puts sweets and other treats in the shoes (or coal if the child's been naughty). He wears a red bishop's get-up, riding a white horse through the sky, and is helped by an impish *Zwarte Piet* (Black Pete).

 Philippines The world's longest Christmas season, called *Pasko* in the native Tagalog. Christmas music and decorations appear as early as September and Christmas decorations don't come down until Three Kings, the first Sunday of the following year.

 Poland People fast for 24 hours until the evening of Christmas Eve. Then they all try to spot the first star (*Gwiazdka* or 'Little Star'). The moment it is sighted, the feast of *Wigilia* can begin. If there's an uneven number of people, it's thought someone will die in the coming year – though it's considered bad luck to invite guests.

 Russia Presents may come from one of two sources. *Ded Moroz* (Grandfather Frost) and his granddaughter travel in a *troika*, a magical sleigh pulled by three horses. But there's also *Babouschka*, the elderly woman who didn't help the Wise Men, who wanders around leaving gifts while searching for the Magi. For most Russians, Christmas is usually January 7th, still going by the Julian calendar. Christmas dinner, meatless, may have 12 courses in honour of the apostles.

Spain Letters asking for gifts are sent by children not to Santa but to the Wise Men, who appear in parades and visit hospitals. Shoes filled with grass or straw are left outside the front door for their camels on Epiphany Eve (January 5th), and gifts appear the following morning.

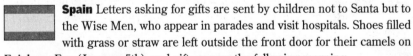 **Venezuela** Between December 16th and 24th there is an early morning church service. In Caracas, it is usual to roller-skate to it so streets are closed to cars until 8am. At bedtime children tie string to their big toe, dangling the other end out of the window: roller-skaters tug the strings as they pass by.

The first appearance of Father Christmas

This famous poem was published anonymously in the *Troy Sentinel* newspaper in 1823, and has been attributed to one Clement Clarke Moore. This is the poem that started it all! Before then, few children outside Holland and Germany had heard of St Nicholas or 'Santa Claus': but on reading the poem they hung up stockings by the chimney, and their parents played along by filling the stockings with treats.

It's perhaps a little syrupy for today's tastes, but it's a great poem to read to children at bedtime on Christmas Eve: it's long enough to lull even the most excitable child to sleep.

'Twas the night before Christmas

'Twas the night before Christmas, when all through the house
  Not a creature was stirring – not even a mouse;
The stockings were hung by the chimney with care,
  In hopes that St Nicholas soon would be there.
The children were nestled all snug in their beds,
  While visions of sugar-plums danced in their heads;
And mamma in her 'kerchief, and I in my cap,
  Had just settled down for a long winter's nap,
When out on the lawn there arose such a clatter,
  I sprang from the bed to see what was the matter.

Away to the window I flew like a flash,
  Tore open the shutters and threw up the sash.
The moon on the breast of the new-fallen snow
  Gave the lustre of mid-day to objects below,
When, what to my wondering eyes should appear,
  But a miniature sleigh, and eight tiny reindeer,
With a little old driver, so lively and quick,
  I knew in a moment it must be St Nick.

More rapid than eagles his coursers they came,
  And he whistled, and shouted, and called them by name;
"Now, Dasher! now, Dancer! now, Prancer and Vixen!
  On, Comet! on, Cupid! on, Donner and Blitzen!

To the top of the porch! to the top of the wall!
Now dash away! dash away! dash away all!"

As dry leaves that before the wild hurricane fly,
When they meet with an obstacle, mount to the sky,
So up to the house-top the coursers they flew,
With the sleigh full of toys, and St Nicholas too.

And then, in a twinkling, I heard on the roof
The prancing and pawing of each little hoof.
As I drew in my hand, and was turning around,
Down the chimney St Nicholas came with a bound.

He was dressed all in fur, from his head to his foot,
And his clothes were all tarnished with ashes and soot;
A bundle of toys he had flung on his back,
And he looked like a peddler just opening his pack.

His eyes – how they twinkled! his dimples how merry!
His cheeks were like roses, his nose like a cherry!
His droll little mouth was drawn up like a bow,
And the beard of his chin was as white as the snow;
The stump of a pipe he held tight in his teeth,
And the smoke it encircled his head like a wreath;
He had a broad face and a little round belly,
That shook, when he laughed like a bowlful of jelly.

He was chubby and plump, a right jolly old elf,
And I laughed when I saw him, in spite of myself;
A wink of his eye and a twist of his head,
Soon gave me to know I had nothing to dread;
He spoke not a word, but went straight to his work,
And filled all the stockings; then turned with a jerk,
And laying his finger aside of his nose,
And giving a nod, up the chimney he rose;
He sprang to his sleigh, to his team gave a whistle,
And away they all flew like the down of a thistle.
But I heard him exclaim, ere he drove out of sight,
"Happy Christmas to all, and to all a good-night."

This illustration by Thomas Nast accompanied the poem in an 1876 edition of Harper's Weekly

Turkey names

Turkeys originated in Mexico and were brought to Europe by the Spanish in the 16th century. The baffling name arose when they were confused with guinea fowl, then known as turkey-cocks because they were imported from Africa through Turkey. Somehow the name stuck.

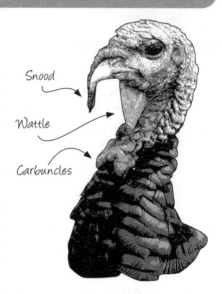

Snood

Wattle

Carbuncles

It isn't only the English who struggled with the provenance of the strange bird. Most languages link it to a country but only Portuguese even manages to place it in the right continent.

Language	Name for turkey	Meaning
Turkish	Hindi	⎫
French	Dinde	⎬ From India
Russian	Indiuk	⎭
Hebrew	Tarnegol Hodu	⎫ Indian chicken
Catalan	Gall Dindi	⎭
Dutch	Kalkoen	⎫
Danish	Kalkun	⎬ Indian (from Calcutta)
Swedish	Kalkon	⎭
Portuguese	Peru	From Peru
Arabic	Dikrumi	Roman bird (sometimes Ethiopian)
Greek	Gallopoula	⎫ French chicken
Gaelic	Cearc Frangais	⎭
Japanese	Shichimencho	Seven-faced bird
Chinese	Huoji	Fire chicken
Malay	Ayam Belanda	Dutch chicken

The Chinese and Japanese names are taken from the ability of the turkey to change the colour of its snood, wattle and carbuncles (see above): these turn bright red when the turkey is either courting or distressed. Since domestic turkeys are unable to mate unaided, these states probably amount to the same thing.

More turkey facts

- Turkeys are believed to have first been brought to Britain in 1526 by Yorkshireman William Strickland – he acquired six birds from American–Indian traders on his travels and sold them for tuppence each in Bristol.

- Henry VIII was the first English king to feast on turkey.

- The first meal eaten by Neil Armstrong and Buzz Aldrin on the moon was cold roast turkey. Did they wear paper hats and blow streamers? NASA isn't telling – another cover-up, no doubt.

- Turkey was a luxury until the 1950s, when fridges and freezers became more commonplace and it was possible to store them.

- The Aztecs, who kept turkeys before the Europeans arrived, called them *xuehxolotl* in the Nahuatl tongue. *Xuehxolotl* with all the trimmings sounds rather more exotic – or it would do if we knew how to pronounce it.

Ban the pud

Strange to think that when you eat your Christmas pudding and mince pies you're breaking the law.

After King Charles I was beheaded in 1649, Cromwell and the Puritans ran the country. They weren't a bundle of laughs and Parliament banned the celebration of saints' days and Christmas, specifically outlawing mince pies, plum puddings and decorations of holly and ivy. It was hard to enforce, though. During the late 1640s, attempts to force shops to stay open and stop people enjoying Christmas led to violent clashes in London, Norwich, Bury St Edmunds and Canterbury.

At the Restoration of the Monarchy in 1660, all legislation enacted during the Protectorate was declared null and void and Christmas could openly be celebrated again. However, we checked with the Law Society, who told us that these laws have never officially been repealed and thus technically remain on the statute book. It makes Christmas pud taste even better, knowing that simply eating it is illegal.

There are plenty of eyebrow-raising laws still in force in Britain, such as the Town Police Clauses Act of 1847. You can still be punished with a £1,000 fine for setting a firework alight, singing a profane or obscene song or ballad or for using *any* profane or obscene language. Also, bizarrely, it is forbidden to "use any slide upon ice or snow". So sledging is out, too.

Merry Christmas and a Happy New Year

Never be lost for a festive greeting again! You don't know who's going to drop in unexpectedly on Christmas Day, so it's best to be prepared.

Afrikaans	Gesëende Kersfees
Arabic	Milad Majid
Argentine	Feliz Navidad
Armenian	Shenoraavor Nor Dari yev Pari Gaghand
Azeri	Tezze Iliniz Yahsi Olsun
Basque	Zorionak eta Urte Berri On
Bohemian	Vesele Vanoce
Brazilian	Boas Festas e Feliz Ano Novo
Breton	Nedeleg Laouen na Bloavezh Mat
Bulgarian	Tchestita Koleda; Tchestito Rojdestvo Hristovo
Chinese	Kung His Hsin Nien bing Chu Shen Tan (Mandarin)
	Gun Tso Sun Tan'Gung Haw Sun (Cantonese)
Cornish	Nadelik Looan na Looan Blethen Noweth
Cree	Mitho Makosi Kesikansi
Croatian	Sretan Bozic
Czech	Prejeme Vam Vesele Vanoce a Stastny Novy Rok
Danish	Glædelig Jul
Dutch	Vrolijk Kerstfeest en een Gelukkig Nieuwjaar
Esperanto	Gajan Kristnaskon
Estonian	Ruumsaid Juulup Hi
Farsi	Cristmas-e-shoma Mobarak Bashad
Finnish	Hyvaa Joulua
French	Joyeux Noel
Frisian	Noflike Krystdagen en in Protte Lok en Seine yn it Nije Jier
German	Froehliche Weihnachten
Greek	Kala Christouyenna
Hawaiian	Mele Kalikimaka
Hebrew	Mo'adim Lesimkha – Chena Tova
Hindi	Shub Naya Baras
Hungarian	Kellemes Karacsonyi Unnepeket
Icelandic	Gledileg Jol
Indonesian	Selamat Hari Natal
Iraqi	Idah Saidan Wa Sanah Jadidah

Irish	Nollaig Shona Dhuit
Italian	Buone Feste Natalizie
Japanese	Shinnen Omedeto – Kurisumasu Omedeto
Korean	Sung Tan Chuk Ha
Latvian	Prieci'gus Ziemsve'tkus un Laimi'gu Jauno Gadu
Lithuanian	Linksmu Kaledu
Maltese	Il-Milied it-tajjeb
Manx	Nollick Ghennal as Blein Vie Noa
Maori	Meri Kirihimete
Marathi	Shub Naya Varsh
Navajo	Merry Keshmish
Norwegian	God Jul
Polish	Wesolych Swiat Bozego Narodzenia
Portuguese	Boas Festas
Rapa-Nui	Mata-Ki-Te-Rangi – Te-Pito-O-Te-Henua
Romanian	Sarbatori Vesele
Romanche	Legreivlas Fiastas da Nadal e Bien Niev Onn
Russian	Pozdrevlyayu s Prazdnikom Rozhdestva is Novim Godom
Sami	Buorrit Juovllat
Samoan	La Maunia le Kilisimasi ma le Tausaga Fou
Scots Gaelic	Nollaig Chridheil Huibh
Serb-Croatian	Sretam Bozic – Vesela Nova Godina
Serbian	Hristos se Rodi
Singhalese	Subha nath Thalak Vewa – Subha Aluth Awrudhak Vewa
Slovakian	Sretan Bozic – Vesele Vianoce
Slovene	Vesele Bozicne – Srecno Novo Leto
Spanish	Feliz Navidad
Swedish	God Jul and (Och) Ett Gott Nytt År
Tagalog	Maligayamg Pasko – Masaganang Bagong Taon
Tamil	Nathar Puthu Varuda Valthukkal
Thai	Sawadee Pee Mai
Turkish	Noeliniz Ve Yeni Yiliniz Kutlu Olsun
Ukrainian	Srozhdestvom Kristovym
Urdu	Naya Saal Mubarak Ho
Vietnamese	Chung Mung Giang Sinh
Welsh	Nadolig Llawen
Yugoslavian	Cestitamo Bozic

The history of the Christmas tree

It may seem a little bizarre to cut down a perfectly healthy tree and bring it indoors for twelve days. But our reverence for winter evergreens is one of mankind's oldest traditions. To mark the winter solstice, the ancient Egyptians brought green date palms into their homes, similarly the Romans brought evergreens during their festival, *Saturnalia*, while Britain's Druids celebrated with holly and mistletoe and put evergreen branches over their doors to ward off evil spirits.

Although it's almost certainly untrue that Martin Luther is credited with first having the idea of decorating a tree with candles, it was the Germans who established the tradition of bringing a fir tree into the house each Christmas and decorating it, although it was a tradition almost entirely restricted to the upper Rhineland until the end of the 18th century.

A Victorian Christmas

Decorated Christmas trees had become popular by the early 19th century in the homes and castles of the European nobility and royalty, but things moved up a stage in Britain when Queen Victoria married German Prince Albert who gave away many trees to schools and army barracks. The famous illustration of the 'Christmas Tree at Windsor Castle', showing the Royals' giant fir in all its splendour, was published in 1848, and started the trend in Britain.

It took longer to spread in the United States, the German tendency towards Christmas celebration being at odds with Puritan attitudes. The Pilgrim Fathers had banned Christmas and even in the 1850s there was a storm when a minister in Cleveland allowed a tree into his church. Until 1870, schools in Boston remained open on Christmas Day. It was a losing battle, though, with the Christmas trees becoming widespread in the United States by the end of the 19th century.

The artificial intervention

The first fake trees were made from goose feathers dyed green. These, too, originated in Germany, and were fashionable in Britain in the 1920s. The more modern fake trees originally came from an American brush company in the early 20th century, made from brush bristles on wire. In the 1950s and 60s, metallic trees made with aluminium-covered paper were all the rage, despite being too much of a fire hazard to have lights anywhere near them; they were often lit by a spotlight with a rotating colour wheel.

Starting to get a little silly

Recently, upside-down trees, hung from the ceiling, have become a minor fad. The manufacturers of one that comes with lights already fitted say that more presents will fit under it and claim that, in the 12th century, fir trees were widely hung upside-down from ceilings at Christmas in Europe.

Even fewer people have opted for the mp3 Christmas tree, a 6ft fibre-optic tree with an mp3 player and speakers in its base!

Mistletoe

Mistletoe is a parasite, much like the guy from accounts who carries a sprig around at the office party, hoping to grab a kiss. It doesn't grow in the ground, but attaches itself to trees, and fruits in winter. To the ancients, it was a sacred plant with miraculous healing powers; enemies who encountered each other beneath it would make a truce until the next day. As a result, it was hung up as a symbol of peace and goodwill.

The habit of kissing under the mistletoe dates back to the Greeks and Romans, though for them it was a sign of betrothal. Its pagan links with fertility – and licentiousness – led the Church to ban it. A little surprisingly, it was the Victorians who reintroduced mistletoe as an excuse for a seasonal snog, though the lady was supposed to remove a berry from the branch for each kiss.

Mistletoe is poisonous. Eating the berries can cause gastroenteritis and may be fatal. So make sure you keep your mouth shut while you're snogging under it.

Looking after your Christmas tree

We confess that until we started researching this, we had no idea that we'd been getting Christmas trees wrong all these years. Dumb and dumber we were because we bought cheap trees locally, brought them straight into the house and then spent most of the next fortnight grumbling about all the pine needles being shed.

These cheap trees are Norwegian spruce (*picea abies*). Pretty they may be, but they are the alopecia sufferers of the Christmas tree family, losing their needles at the drop of a hat – which means that if Uncle Bernie does his usual post-prandial snoring, you'll have to mount a massive mop-up operation.

You may have to go a little further than your local supermarket car park but, far better at needle retention are trees like the Nordman Fir (*abies nordmanniana*), the Noble Fir (*abies procera*), Scots Pine (*pinus sylvestris*), Douglas Fir (*pseudotsuga menziesii* – has a lovely citrusy smell) and Fraser Fir (*abies fraseri*).

Many trees are cut in October and then put in cold storage until December. These early-harvested trees drop needles far more readily than trees cut closer to Christmas. You'll pay more for the fresh ones, but do you really want to spend much of the holidays clearing up those pesky needles? The needles and branches should bend but not break and if you shake a tree or bang it gently on its stump, you shouldn't see needles cascading off like a nasty case of dandruff. Ensure you have enough clear stump at the bottom to fit the tree into your stand without major surgery and get a tree at least a foot shorter than the room it's going to stand in.

Trees don't like centrally heated homes so, if you can, store yours outside until you need it. Put it in some water and away from the wind and sun. Just before you bring it inside, saw an inch or so off the base of the trunk to open up the pores.

Hoe, hoe, hoe!

Knock it on the ground gently to shake off those needles that are just about to fall.

Once inside, treat a tree much like cut flowers, keeping the base in water. Although some people swear to the benefits of adding sugar or aspirin, plain water is best. Keep it topped up. It will need a lot; when it's cut down, half its weight is water! If you haven't got a stand that will hold water, jam it upright in a bucket with stones or even scrunched-up newspaper. Siting the tree away from fires and radiators will help too. If the water dries up, the tree will form a sap seal over the stump and it won't absorb any more water.

Remarkably, the length of time you can keep a Christmas tree indoors before it begins to deteriorate is about… 12 days!

In these environmentally conscious times, many wonder about the merits of felling trees to decorate our homes for less than a fortnight. Isn't it better to get an artificial tree that you can use for years? Swedish researchers compared the energy involved in cutting and transporting a real tree to the manufacture and importation of a plastic tree from the Far East that was used for 10 years and then thrown into a landfill. The plastic one was five times as 'costly' to the environment. Hmm… Sweden? Isn't that where lots of Christmas trees come from?

Although there are concerns about the lack of biodiversity with so many Christmas trees being grown, the Consumers' Association found that many tree plantations have a beneficial effect on wildlife, with one Welsh conifer plantation playing home to 300 pairs of willow warblers, 15 times that on the same area of agricultural farmland. Ahh!

Jeremiah's diatribe

The *Old Testament* prophet Jeremiah wasn't known for his sense of fun. Centuries before the appearance of Christianity, he expressed his disapproval for the pagan custom of cutting down trees, bringing them indoors and decorating them:

> Thus saith the LORD, Learn not the way of the heathen, and be not dismayed at the signs of heaven; for the heathen are dismayed at them. For the customs of the people are vain: for one cutteth a tree out of the forest, the work of the hands of the workman, with the axe. They deck it with silver and with gold; they fasten it with nails and with hammers, that it move not. *Jeremiah 10:2-4*

Christmas trees may be an old tradition, but there have always been those who disapprove of frivolity.

The first Christmas card

In 2001 a Christmas card was sold at auction for £20,000. It had been sent in 1843 by Sir Henry Cole, the first director of the Victoria and Albert museum, to his grandmother. So why all the fuss?

It wasn't only the celebrity status of the sender. For Sir Henry had commissioned his friend, the noted artist John Calcott Horsley, to design the card: a batch of 1,000 were printed, which were then hand coloured and sold for a shilling each at a shop in London's New Bond Street. Cole hadn't just produced a Christmas innovation, he'd started an entire industry that's now worth an astonishing £1.5 billion a year.

Only 10 of that original printing are still in existence. Another, which had been sent to one Mary Tripsack (a friend of the poet Elizabeth Barrett Browning), was sold in 2005 for £8,469 to Jakki Brown, the general secretary of the Greeting Card Association. As she later put it: "There are a lot of people out there who feel they owe their livelihoods to Sir Henry Cole."

The first known published Christmas card (1843) by artist John Calcott Horsley, reproduced by kind permission of the Hallmark Archives, Hallmark Cards, Inc.

Boxing Day

The day after Christmas is celebrated as Boxing Day in Britain and its former dominions, although the term is largely unknown in the rest of the world.

The reason for its curious name is long forgotten, although it has nothing to do with having to dispose of all that unnecessary packaging from Christmas presents nor with the fights that break out over whose toys belong to whom.

Originally St Stephen's Day (when Good King Wenceslas looked out), this was the day on which the toffs gave presents to their staff and tradesmen. Were the presents given out in boxes?

What's in the box?

I hope it's an mp3 Christmas tree

These days, Boxing Day is a big day for sport. Once restricted to playing fields, the competitive spirit has now spread to the nation's stores as people who have spent Christmas night huddled in sleeping bags on the pavement fight each other for juicy bargains in the winter sales.

One Boxing Day tradition that hasn't survived is the Hunting of the Wren. From Neolithic times on, the wren was considered the king of birds around Europe and, as such, it was unlucky to kill one. An exception was made on Boxing Day when groups of boys would do just that. Sticking the dead bird on a pole decorated with ribbons and holly, they'd blacken their faces and go from house to house after money or gifts, singing this jolly song:

The wren, the wren, the king of all birds,
On St Stephen's Day was caught in the furze,
Up with the penny and down with the pan,
Give us a penny to bury the wren.

Suddenly, having them spending Boxing Day sitting in front of the TV playing computer games doesn't seem so bad.

You're Nicked: the origins of Santa

How exactly did a 4th-century Turkish bishop get transformed into the rotund, red-cheeked, jovial, bewhiskered, sleigh-riding, ho-ho-hoing old gent who personifies Christmas today?

St Nicholas of Myra, a bishop from the age of 17 in what's now Turkey, was well known for giving presents to the poor, his most renowned gift being

dowries to the three impoverished daughters of a devout Christian so they wouldn't need to turn to prostitution. He is said to have thrown one of the three bags of gold down a chimney into a stocking drying there. Oddly, though, St Nicholas is *not* a real saint. There's no record he was ever canonised, and the Pope removed him from the calendar of saints in 1969.

All this got mixed in with folklore from various nations over the years, the most influential being the Dutch. While other Protestant countries shunned saints days, as a big trading nation the Dutch continued to celebrate St Nicholas's Day, for St Nicholas was the patron saint of sailors, among other things.

The Dutch portrayed *Sinterklaas*, as they called him, with a long white beard and red and white ecclesiastical robes. It was in America that he was transformed into Santa – although 'Santa Claus' is actually a perpetuation of a mishearing by linguistically challenged English settlers in New Amsterdam (later New York) of the Dutch name.

Our modern ideas of Father Christmas owe much to the poem *'Twas the Night Before Christmas* (see page 42), which first gave him the ample belly and eight reindeer, as well as to the 19th-century drawings of *Harper's Weekly* cartoonist Thomas Nast.

Advertising for Coca-Cola in the 1930s that showed Santa enjoying a bottle of the stuff was responsible for a recent urban myth that Coke's artists invented Santa. In fact, the modern idea of a sack-carrying, red-garbed, jolly Santa was already well in place a decade or two earlier. It is true, however, that a reindeer called Rudolph with a red nose was invented in 1939 as a promotional gimmick for the Montgomery Ward chain of department stores.

To begin to toboggan

To begin to toboggan
First buy a toboggan
But don't buy too big a toboggan.
Too big a toboggan
Is not a toboggan
To buy to begin to toboggan.

I'm going elf for leather

Accidents at Christmas

If there's one tradition that never fails to make an appearance at Christmas, it's that of accidents. The twelve days see some 80,000 accidents at home requiring a trip to hospital. According to the Royal Society for the Prevention of Accidents, not all are down to arguments over who won the wishbone.

Embarrassed patients have to explain that they missed their chair when they tried to sit down for their meal, that they stabbed themselves with scissors they were using to assemble toys, that they fell over new toys or the cables of the new computer, that the gravy exploded in the microwave or that they've been burnt by hot turkey fat.

One thousand people have mishaps with Christmas trees each year – many just trying to carry the things home – another 1,000 incur Christmas decoration-related injuries, many caused by Christmas tree lights: either falling when putting them up, inadvertently swallowing the bulbs or getting electric shocks from old or cheap lights.

Cut the risk. Use screwdrivers, not scissors to put new toys together and to change plugs. Open packaging with scissors, not your sharpest kitchen knife. Christmas trees – particularly those harvested early – are a very real fire hazard so keep them watered and turn off the lights when you're not around. Never use electric lights on a metal or metallic-framed tree and don't leave candles burning when you're not there to watch them.

If you want something useful this Christmas, buy yourself a fire extinguisher. Many of them come in lovely Christmas colours.

Great Christmas films

For many, the true spirit of Christmas means lying slumped in front of the television. But it isn't all seasonal rubbish: some of the greatest films ever made are about Christmas, and many of them are broadcast at this time of year.

Here are some of the better examples of yuletide fare, together with some interesting facts and trivia about the movies with which you can amaze and astound your family and friends.

The Thin Man (1934)

A routine detective story is turned into cinematic joy by fantastic verbal sparring from William Powell and Myrna Loy as hard-drinking, wisecracking, affectionate Nick and Nora. They set the standard for all other movie couples to follow.

The original book was written by Dashiell Hammett, whose most famous detective was Sam Spade (*The Maltese Falcon*). It's his picture on the cover of *The Thin Man* novel shown during the opening credits.

The Thin Man isn't Nick Charles, the detective, but Clyde Wynant, the murder victim. The wirehaired terrier Asta (played by Skippy) was so popular he started off a craze for the breed. As well as appearing in the other Thin Man films, the dog also starred in *Bringing Up Baby* and *The Awful Truth*.

The Shop Around the Corner (1940)

This delightful Ernst Lubitsch comedy stars James Stewart and Margaret Sullivan as colleagues working in a shoe shop ahead of Christmas who loathe each other, not realising that they are actually pen pals.

It was later remade as the musical *In the Good Old Summertime* and the lamentable *You've Got Mail*. The Hungarian play on which the film was based was also the basis for the award-winning stage musical, *She Loves Me*.

It's a Wonderful Life (1946)

This deliciously sentimental favourite, with James Stewart as a 'failure' who discovers what his suicide would mean to his home town, is probably the only movie to be made from a Christmas card. Writer Philip Van Doren Stern used the story on his cards one year and got such a good response from his friends that it was published.

The film was initially a flop at the box office, losing over half a million dollars. It was only when it was picked up as a seasonal offering for TV that it gained popularity. Director Frank Capra didn't benefit, though, as the copyright had lapsed and had not been renewed.

It's one of the loveliest, kindliest, happiest and most emotional films ever made, even if it is a little stilted in places now and hard to get sceptical modern kids to sit through. Nonetheless, by the end, you're so glad to be alive you want to go round and hug everyone.

Miracle on 34th Street (1947)

The ultimate Christmas movie, with Edmund Gwenn a department store Santa who claims to be the real Father Christmas. Sweet and charming, it has several scenes that are pure movie magic, unlike the inferior remake.

This wasn't originally a Christmas movie. Although filmed around Christmas of 1946 with the full cooperation of Macy's department store, the studio didn't think much of the result and so released it in June 1947 at the height of summer. Despite this, it was a big hit.

Scrooge (1951)

Known in America as *A Christmas Carol*, this faithful rendition is surely the best of all the many versions of Dickens' story. After seeing it, it's hard to imagine anyone other than goggle-eyed Alastair Sim as Ebenezer Scrooge ever again.

White Christmas (1954)

This perennial favourite starring Bing Crosby and Danny Kaye is a virtual remake of the 1942 film *Holiday Inn*. Two old army buddies team up to try to save a ski lodge owned by their former commander. It's a sickly confection of schmaltzy fluff, but most bits of fluff don't have a top-notch set of songs by Irving Berlin to keep them aloft.

The original idea was to reunite Crosby with Fred Astaire but Astaire refused, claiming he had retired (although he did go on to make other films). Donald

O'Connor was cast but pulled out at the last moment. The famous *Sisters* number was inserted after the director saw Kaye and Crosby doing it when they were goofing around.

You may think you know the film well, but if you don't know *Abraham*, that's because it's usually cut out of TV screenings these days. A blackface musical number doesn't go down too well.

The Sound of Music (1965)

What would Christmas be without a helping of the *Sound of Music* (or *The Sound of Mucus*, as Christopher Plummer referred to it)? Naughty novice nun Maria (Julie Andrews) becomes governess to an uptight widower and his brood of pre-Osmond singing angels. Cue for *Do-Re-Mi*, *My Favorite Things* and *Edelweiss*. If only it weren't for those pesky Nazis.

Alfred Hitchcock called it "the most evil film to ever come out of Hollywood", while Plummer said that working with Andrews was "like being hit over the head with a Valentine's card". A Korean distributor thought the film was too long – so he cut all the songs out.

Marni Nixon, the singing marvel who dubbed the stars for *My Fair Lady*, *The King and I* and *West Side Story* appears on screen for the only time as Sister Sophia. Christopher Plummer initially refused to be dubbed – until they played his singing back to him.

Geographically savvy viewers have pointed out that the mountains the Von Trapps flee across are taking them into Germany, not Switzerland. Just because you can sing, it doesn't mean you know jack about geography.

Gremlins (1984)

Billy gets given a cuddly critter from Creatures-R-Us for Christmas. If only he paid attention to the instructions. "Keep him out of the light… don't get him wet. And never, never feed him after midnight." A great comedy horror that actually provides laughs as well as thrills. Writer Chris Columbus thought up the film after dreaming that mice were nibbling his fingers.

Die Hard (1988)

"Welcome to the party, pal." One of the great action thrillers, the more you watch this Christmas-set movie the cleverer you realise it is. As well as Bruce Willis as cop-turned-avenging angel, Alan Rickman is excellent in hissable panto mode as the villain of the piece. The ill-fated building is actually 20th Century Fox tower, headquarters of the company that made the film.

Home Alone (1990)

When the massed ranks of the McCallister family head to Paris for Christmas, they only forget one thing – Kevin. Accidentally left alone by his parents, he finds his home the target of a pair of incompetent burglars. One of the most popular of all comedies at the time, this piece of modern slapstick has endured and become a perennial Christmas favourite.

Writer John Hughes was inspired to write the story after briefly losing one of his own children in a department store. There are plenty of enjoyable gaffes in the movie: look out for Mom flying home from Paris; she arrives on a different type of plane to the one she left on. Joe Pesci also forgets which hand he has burnt on the hot doorknob.

The Nightmare Before Christmas (1993)

Jack Skellington, king of Halloween Town, discovers Christmas and tries to get his own ghostly and ghastly residents to celebrate it. Tim Burton's wonderfully imaginative stop-motion animation is bizarre and beautiful, often very funny and has some splendidly twisted songs.

I was this close to getting the part!

Elf (2003)

Will Farrell, raised among Santa's elves, sets off to find his real dad, curmudgeonly James Caan! What could have been awful and twee turned out to be a triumph, hilariously funny without the sentiment ever going too far over the top. Very much in the mould of classic family Christmas movies.

Christmas books

This is the season to make even the most respected authors go a little soft around the edges. Here's a selection of some of the more entertaining yuletide fare.

A Christmas Carol
Charles Dickens
Curmudgeonly old miser Ebenezer Scrooge is visited by ghosts, sees the error of his ways, and spawns 37 movies and TV adaptations.

Hercule Poirot's Christmas
Agatha Christie
Curmudgeonly old miser Simeon Lee calls all his family together, all of whom have a good reason for wishing him dead. Surprise, surprise! He gets murdered.

The Adventure of the Christmas Pudding
Agatha Christie
Curmudgeonly detective Hercule Poirot finds more red herrings than currants on his plate as he's warned not to eat the pudding.

A Highland Christmas
M C Beaton
Curmudgeonly detective Hamish Macbeth employs all his detecting skills to find out who stole the Christmas lights from the town of Lochdubh. That rare thing – a detective story with no murders.

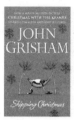

Skipping Christmas
John Grisham
Curmudgeonly old accountant Luther Krank estimates how much his family spent on Christmas last year, and this year books a Caribbean cruise instead.

How the Grinch Stole Christmas
Dr Seuss
Curmudgeonly old monster tries to sabotage the festive season by kidnapping Santa. Charged verse from the master of children's writing.

Delia Smith's Christmas
Delia Smith
Curmudgeonly celebrity chef assembles a slew of mysterious ingredients as the festive turkey meets its grisly fate. Minimal character development, but some mouth-watering descriptions of food.

Father Christmas
Raymond Briggs
Curmudgeonly philanthropist Santa Claus awakes from his dream of summer to find that it's Christmas Eve. Will he manage to deliver presents to all the children in time? Well, what do you think?

First Noel
Jan Pieńkowski
Curmudgeonly paper engineer Jan Pieńkowski tries desperately to follow up his earlier *Haunted House* success with a text from the Bible and a book that opens out into a carousel Christmas decoration.

Sharpe's Christmas
Bernard Cornwell
Curmudgeonly military author Cornwell is commissioned to write two 12,000 word seasonal stories for the *Daily Mail*, and decides to make some seasonal cash by publishing them in a *very* slim book.

Shakespeare's Christmas
Charlaine Harris
Curmudgeonly cleaning lady Lily Bard survives a gang rape and attempted murder, and ends up solving a mystery in her home town of Shakespeare, Arkansas.

Christmas at Stalingrad
Antony Beevor
When the curmudgeonly German 6th Army is surrounded by Russian troops in Stalingrad on Christmas Eve, they keep their spirits up by singing *Silent Night*.

A Redbird Christmas
Fannie Flagg
Curmudgeonly down and out Oswald T Campbell has only a few months to live unless he leaves wintry Chicago for the deep South. Trailer park misfits for all occasions.

The Christmas Thief
Mary and Carol Higgins Clark
Curmudgeonly detective Regan Reilly teams up with lottery winner Alvirah Meehan to track down a 90-foot hijacked tree that Maria von Trapp used to sing beneath, and which also contains a hoard of stolen jewellery.

Fill My Stocking: A Christmas Anthology
Alan Titchmarsh
Stories, poems, watercolours and anecdotes from the green-fingered TV celebrity who, unusually, doesn't seem to be at all curmudgeonly.

Victoria's Christmas blowout

Think you feel stuffed after turkey and trimmings? Then spare a thought for Queen Victoria and her entourage, who waded through course after course at festive banquets. The menu here was served on Christmas Day at her home, Osborne House, in 1896. It's a little hard to read, so let us detail the contents for you.

The meal kicked off with *La Tête de Veau en Tortue*, which is a calf's head cooked 'tortoise style'. As well as a whole, de-brained and de-tongued calf's head, the recipe included 24 truffles, 12 crayfish and 12 fried eggs. Oh, and four calf ears, although how they got four ears from a single head is anyone's guess.

The second course was a choice of turbot in Hollandaise sauce, or a plain fillet of sole; enough to give them a taste for the entrée, *Les Kromeskys à la Toulouse*. Kromeskys turn out to be Polish croquettes of minced beef, and the Toulouse element is clearly just the chef having a laugh.

On to the main course: a choice of roast sirloin of beef, chine of pork (a special Italian fillet) or, at long last, *Les Dindes rôties à la Chipolata* – that's turkey and chipolatas, to you and me. Followed, naturally, by plum pudding.

It's all rounded off with a choice of desserts: asparagus, good old mince pies, or *Le Pain de riz à la cintra* – which we can only translate as curved rice bread. This one probably tastes better than it sounds.

But even this gargantuan feast clearly wasn't enough to satisfy Victorian appetites. Just in case anyone felt a bit peckish between courses, there was a side table containing brawn, a woodcock pie, a wild boar's head and a game pie. And a baron of beef as well. Phew! And they couldn't even fall asleep during the Queen's Christmas message!

4 Do it yourself

IF YOU PUT YOUR MIND TO IT you can order your entire Christmas online, without even getting out of your chair: decorations, crackers, even an entire Christmas meal neatly arranged on a microwave-ready plastic tray.

But let's face it, that would make for a pretty miserable Christmas for you and your family. You may well spend the rest of the year in an internet-induced stupor, but this is the one time of year when you need to dig out the old *Blue Peter* kit of glue, tape and sticky back plastic, and start assembling things.

Making decorations is easy, fun, and an excellent way to keep kids entertained in that frenzied run-up period when they ask you every five minutes how long it is until Christmas. Here are some interesting designs – including an indoor snowman that's guaranteed never to melt.

As well as 3D nativity scenes, and an interesting napkin fold to liven up your table, we'll also show you how you can make your own crackers from scratch, with a selection of jokes ready for you to cut out and insert into each one.

The napkin rose

One of our favourite napkin folds, this one's a little tricky to do but well worth the effort. After the final step shown here you can shape the whole thing until it's almost spherical, and even serve tiny delicacies in it. Let's see the Joneses try to keep up with *this* one!

This design works well with either well-starched linen napkins, or the heavier duty paper variety. Very flimsy paper napkins will simply tend to tear when you try some of the more complex folds.

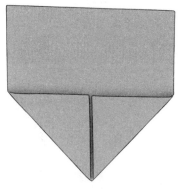

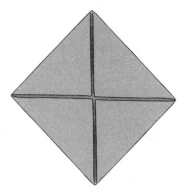

1 Lay your napkin out flat on the table. Fold one corner into the middle, then another corner. Flatten the creases.

2 Continue folding until all four corners meet in the middle. Remember to keep flattening each crease!

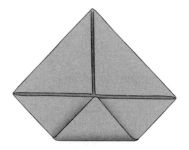

3 Fold one corner into the middle (and flatten that crease).

4 Fold all the new corners into the middle of the napkin.

5 Now turn the whole assembly over to work on the other side.

6 Fold one corner into the middle – and flatten that crease!

7 Now fold all the rest of the corners into the middle.

8 Now, reach underneath the napkin…

9 … and pull out one of the corners beneath. You'll need to hold the centre of the napkin down with the other hand.

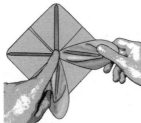

10 Rotate the napkin 90°, still holding the centre with your other hand, and pull out the next corner.

11 Continue until all four underneath corners have been pulled out.

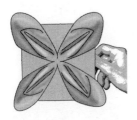

12 Now, rotate the napkin 45° and reach beneath it…

13 … and pull out the flap beneath.

14 Pull out all the flaps, and bend into a cup shape.

How to make an indoor snowman

Everyone loves a snowman. The trouble is, you have to wait for it to snow – and then, after hours of painstaking modelling, you know the poor thing's going to turn to slush as soon as there's a warm spell.

Our solution is a do-it-yourself snowman that will last for ever, and it can even be brought indoors. You can make this one any size you like, up to a fantastic 4ft high. The trick: it's not made of snow (you'd probably already guessed that), but a sheet of 4ft x 4ft polystyrene, of the sort sold for insulation in building supplies and DIY shops.

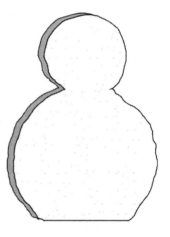

1 Begin by cutting a snowman shape out of the sheet of polystyrene. A serrated knife works well for this. No need to be too accurate: a rough edge is more lifelike!

2 Now use the rest of the sheet to make three or four more snowman outlines, each one an inch or two smaller than the first. If you want to do the back as well – and you don't have to – then you'll need to make two of each new set of shapes.

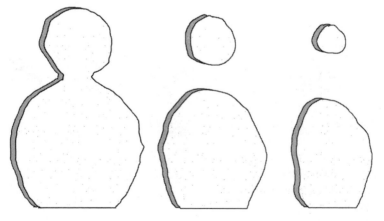

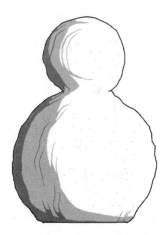

3 Place the cutouts on top of the original to form the contours of the finished snowman. Glue them in place using polystyrene ceiling tile glue (or just hold them with screws).

4 Now use the knife to chamfer all the edges, or just crumble them away with your fingers, until you get a smooth three-dimensional snowman shape. This can take some time!

5 Now you can decorate your snowman as you would the real thing – with a hat, a scarf, a carrot for the nose, and so on. You can glue in chestnuts for the eyes, but you may find it easier to draw a mouth on with a felt pen.

Here's the clever part: you'll have lots of bits of polystyrene left over, particularly if you crumbled the edges away in step 4. Don't throw them away: piled up around the base, they look exactly like snow! While this snowman may blow away outdoors, it will look great sitting in your hallway.

Can you smell carrot?

The advent star

Fans of *Blue Peter* will remember this one: John Noakes used to create it every year without fail. In those far-off times, his version included real candles – we lived close to the edge in those days!

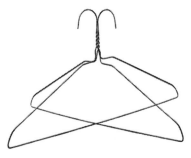

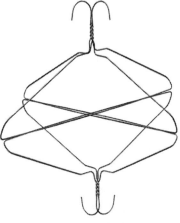

1 Begin by attaching two coat hangers at right angles, going through each other. Fix together using tape or wire.

2 Now add two more hangers, similarly attached upside down (above right).

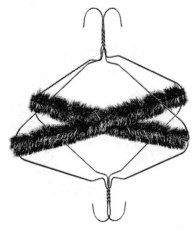

3 Fix tinsel to the two cross pieces to mask the joins and help to hold the whole thing together.

4 Add holly, baubles and other Christmas decorations hanging from the star. And that's it!

Holly wreath

A surprisingly easy decoration to make, as long as you can lay your hands on some holly. The trick here is to make the frame out of an old wire coat hanger: leave the hook on, as you can use this to hang the finished item on your door.

1 First, squeeze the outer corners of the coat hanger to make a rough diamond shape.

2 Now bend the three corners towards each other to shape the hanger into more of a circle.

3 Take some sprigs of holly and wind them around the coat hanger. It should stay in place by itself.

4 Add some more holly, then wire on a few Christmas baubles left over from the tree.

Rosie's spice bags

As well as the taste and sight of Christmas, don't forget you can nourish the nostrils too. Our friend Rosie conjures up lovely fragrant spice and lavender bags each year that are pretty simple to make.

As long as you can sew, or use a machine, it's not too tricky. For the spice bags, use something like linen which is porous enough for the odours to escape but not so loose that bits will drop out. For the lavender bags, denser material like satin or velvet is better, or else use scraps of old clothes. Aim for bags with sides roughly 4in x 4in.

In the spice bags put whole cloves, broken-up cinnamon sticks and bay leaves, powdered ginger, powdered cinnamon, oil of orange and orris root (used in pot-pourri). Then sew up the bags and, when you want to use them, plonk them on a radiator. As the heating comes on, the bags will emit their splendid fragrance. From time to time, crunch the bags up in your hands to get them going again.

If you can't – or won't – sew, then use a square of material and place all the ingredients in a pile in the middle. Bend all the corners to the top, then simply tie it together with a piece of string.

The lavender bags simply contain dried lavender. If you can't find any locally, it can easily be bought on the internet. The bags are a great way of pepping up presents and giving them that little something extra. If you want to write on the bags, use fabric paint.

Rosie's fruity garlands

Although you can buy garlands in the shops, they're expensive and far less satisfying than making your own. They're also the sort of things kids might want to make with you. Rosie makes them with dried oranges (whole and sliced), apples, chillis and even artichokes, bay leaves, cinnamon sticks and whole nutmegs.

You can try drying oranges and chillis in a very, very low oven but as even Rosie – after years of experience – still burns them, it's probably easier just to buy them already dried. Again, the internet is a good source if you have no supplier conveniently nearby.

All you want from the orange is the skin, so cut slots in them from top to bottom. Oranges become a great decorative feature when cut in this way.

Make a hole in each piece and pass a piece of wire or garden twine through, first tying it at the end to stop everything falling off. Ideally you'd string it on raffia, but this is so fiddly to get it through the holes that it hardly seems worth the bother. Instead, use raffia to disguise the wire or twine, with a few bows of raffia or ribbon at intervals along the garland to break up the other elements.

Once made, these garlands should serve you for years.

Make your own Christmas cracker

Shop-bought crackers are all very well – but the jokes are awful, and the stuff inside is usually rubbish. Far better to make your own: you can fill them with anything from toy cars to pearl earrings, depending on your budget (and, of course, who you're giving them to).

Remember, though, that each cracker is pulled by two people, and you don't know who will win the prize – so unless you're happy for your partner to end up with a plastic statue of Wayne Rooney while your nephew gets two tickets to Paris, you'd better play safe with the gifts.

1 Begin by taking three cardboard loo roll holders, and lay them end to end. Two of them will be removed later – they're just to form the shape.

2 Tape a cracker snap to the centre holder. These are readily available online, but if you can't find one, get everyone to say 'bang!' when they pull it instead.

3 Cut some crêpe paper or thin wrapping paper large enough to fit around all three loo roll holders. Don't use foil paper, as it won't tear when it's pulled – you don't want to give Aunt Emily another hernia.

4 Wrap the paper all the way around the tubes to form a complete loop. Add a piece of tape in the middle to hold it in place.

5 Place a rubber band (or tie a piece of thin string) between two of the cardboard tubes, sliding the end one out a little way as you do so. When this is done, turn the cracker up and drop your prize and joke inside. And you can add a paper hat if you really insist.

6 Slide a rubber band over this other end in a similar way. You should now be able to remove the two end tubes without the paper collapsing. Adding one of those foil bows designed to go on presents adds a festive touch. Your cracker is now complete, and ready for the table!

A couple of things to make sure of: firstly, check that whatever prizes you want to include will actually fit inside the loo roll tube. And secondly, you'll need a plentiful stock of cracker jokes. If you don't feel up to making them up, we've printed a selection overleaf that you can photocopy and cut out.

The instructions here are for a standard, cracker-sized cracker. But of course you don't need to limit yourself: you can make them any size you want, as long as you have suitable tubes. You could use an empty plastic mineral water bottle for a family-sized cracker. And if you have a friend who works in a carpet shop, remember that carpets come wrapped around *really* big cardboard tubes…

Cracker jokes

Making your own crackers? Photocopy this page of jokes, cut them up and put one in each cracker (see previous page). Or just pass them around the table!

What's pink and wobbly and flies?
A jellycopter.

What's ET short for?
Because he only has little legs.

What did the turkey play
in the pop band?
*Percussion – he was the only one
with drumsticks.*

What do you get when you cross a
snowman with a vampire?
Frostbite.

What do you get if you cross an
apple with a Christmas tree?
A pineapple.

What's the difference between
a weasel and a stoat?
*A weasel is weasally recognised and
a stoat is stoatally different.*

What's orange and sounds
like a parrot?
A carrot.

Where does Santa Claus sleep
when he's travelling?
In a ho-ho-hotel.

What bird always succeeds?
A budgie with no teeth.

How long does a candle take
to burn down?
About a wick.

Who beats his chest and
swings from Christmas cake to
Christmas cake?
Tarzipan.

What happens when a hyena
swallows an Oxo cube?
It makes a laughing-stock of itself.

What's yellow and writes poetry?
A ballpoint banana.

What's Christmas called in the UK?
Yule Britannia.

What's red and invisible?

No tomatoes.

How did King Wenceslas like his pizza?

Deep pan, crisp and even.

Where did Napoleon keep his armies?

Up his sleevies.

What did the grape say when the elephant trod on it?

Nothing, it just let out a little wine.

How many crime writers does it take to change a light bulb?

Only one, but it has to have a really good twist at the end.

What's the difference between Santa and a warm dog?

Santa wears a red suit and the dog just pants.

How many people with no sense of humour does it take to change a light bulb?

One.

What happened when the ship carrying red paint collided with the one carrying blue paint?

The sailors were all marooned.

Why is Santa's little helper depressed?

Because he has low elf esteem.

Did you hear about the man who drowned while eating muesli?

He was dragged down by a strong currant.

Which cheese never tells the truth?

Lychees.

What do you call people who are afraid of Santa Claus?

Claustrophobic.

What's a sheep's favourite Christmas carol?

We wish ewe a merry Christmas.

What's Tarzan's favourite Christmas song?

Jungle Bells.

Why did the archaeologist go bankrupt?

Because his career was in ruins.

What's grey, yellow, grey, yellow, grey, yellow, grey, yellow, grey, yellow?

An elephant rolling down a hill with a dandelion in its mouth.

Away in a manger

If you find those plastic nativity figures just too tacky for words, here's a simple way to make a three-dimensional manger scene from any suitable painting. The only trouble is, you'll need three or four copies of it: so unless several of your friends have all happened to send you the same classical Christmas card, you may prefer to photocopy the facing page a few times, enlarging it if you like. It was painted by Marten de Vos in 1577, and is perfect for colouring in.

It works best if you glue all the photocopies onto sheets of thin card first, as paper by itself tends to go a little floppy. All you have to do now is cut out successive planes from the picture. So here, we started by cutting away the view seen behind the cow, donkey, stable and the figure of Joseph, and placing this image on top of the full original.

On a third copy, cut out a smaller foreground area: here, we've removed the cow, donkey and Joseph, leaving just Mary, the angels and the crib on view. Our fourth copy holds just one angel, and the crib.

You now need to fix all these pieces together. The key here is to add some spacing between all the layers: those double-sided sticky pads work well, or you can simply make loops of tape wrapped around cardboard spacers if you prefer.

When seen from the side, as shown here, you see multiple versions of the picture: but when it's viewed head-on, you get a truly three-dimensional version of the image. Try it with other pictures: just make sure you choose images that have clearly defined foreground and background areas.

Stand-up Christmas

This decoration is easy to make out of scraps of cardboard, covered with last year's cast-off wrapping paper. It's a star that will stand up by itself on a table, or can be hung from the tree.

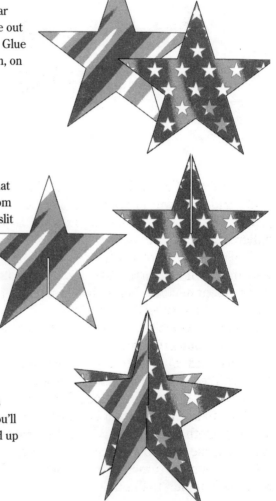

1 Cut two five-pointed star shapes of the same size out of cardboard or stiff paper. Glue foil wrapping paper to them, on both sides.

2 Cut a slit in one star that goes up from the bottom towards the middle, and a slit in the other star that goes down from a point, again towards the middle of the star.

3 Now slide the two slits into each other, and you'll get a 3D star that will stand up on its own.

5 Weird and wonderful

IT'S A STRANGE TIME OF YEAR, Christmas. All that enforced jollity and goodwill is bound to have an effect. It's turned some people's heads more than others: we'll expose some of the more ludicrous offerings in this chapter.

We'll meet the man who celebrates Christmas every day, and visit the town of North Pole, Alaska. We'll examine why the UK government decided Christmas was too scary for children in 2005, and look at the specialist wing of the North American Air Defense Command, which is charged with tracking Santa's airborne progress around the world.

We'll find out what Isaac Newton, Humphrey Bogart and Marcus Trescothick have in common, and why Christmas Day was bad news for both Charlie Chaplin and W C Fields.

Armchair scientists will be interested in the physics of Santa's delivery method, and the proven best method to open a cracker. And for those with an interest in nostalgia, we present the definitive list of Christmas Number One singles, and the toys we broke while we were listening to them.

Photograph: Khanjan Mehta

Will the real Santa please stand up

There *is* a Santa Claus, and North Pole *is* his address.

North Pole, Alaska, that is. You won't see any elves around, but that's where Kris Kringel lives, the name that's synonymous with Santa Claus in America. He's a large guy in his 50s with a long, grey-white beard whose driving licence confirms his name, changed from Charlie Livingston a decade or so ago.

The 'city' (pop. 1,659) is actually 1,700 miles south of the real North Pole and isn't even within the Arctic Circle. The name was chosen in 1953 in the hope it would attract manufacturers excited about the idea of truthfully putting 'Made at North Pole' on toys. It didn't. But an Air Force base was built nearby and then a couple of oil refineries, so the town survived and now has plenty of Santa-mad tourists in the summer. In the town "where the spirit of Christmas lives year round", the mayor keeps Christmas decorations up permanently, the street lights are painted with red and white stripes, many buildings are decked in Christmas colours and streets have names like Saint Nicholas Drive, Donner Drive, Blitzen Drive and Snowman Lane.

Just like most other towns, there's a McDonalds, a Wendys, a Pizza Hut and a Blockbuster. But not many places have a 40ft high fibreglass Father Christmas figure with a 33ft waist.

For $7.50 plus 50c postage, you can get an "Original Letter from Santa". This is the town's best-selling item, and about 100,000 of these are sent around the world each Christmas, all with a genuine North Pole postmark.

Kris changed his name when he got a job at the Santa Claus House, where he greets visitors and has his picture taken. On his days off or when there aren't enough tourists to "Ho, Ho, Ho" to, he apparently delivers pizzas or works in his taxidermy shop, preserving the trophies of local hunters. If you ask for a stuffed animal from *this* Father Christmas, who knows what you'll get.

The terror of Santa

In 2005 a UK government website advised teachers to protect their pupils from the scary effect of having a Santa appear at any Christmas parties because "For very young children, Father Christmas can be terrifying."

They were also warned to be wary of pantomimes, another potential psychological 'scene of crime'. According to advice on *teachernet.gov.uk*, run by the Department for Education and Skills, such scary events could only be contemplated if nervous children were placed near an exit and the lighting was not too dark and atmospheric.

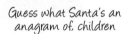

Guess what Santa's an anagram of, children

The advice included suggestions for non-competitive games (what sort of Christmas is *that?*), recommended that children give 'experiences' rather than Christmas presents, only decorate reusable plastic trees and send electronic cards rather than paper ones to cut waste. A present such as breakfast in bed has "far more meaning and doesn't come surrounded by useless packaging".

The noise of cynical laughter was so loud it could clearly be heard in Whitehall. The advice was quickly whipped off the website, with the DfES claiming it didn't represent official policy but that of unspecified 'advisers', and stating: "We fully support the traditional British Christmas." The Prime Minister wouldn't be drawn into the controversy, however, so we still don't know on which side of the Santa believe-disbelieve fence he stands.

Tracking Santa

On Christmas Eve 1955, Sears Roebuck in Colorado misprinted a phone number in an ad. Children who wanted to "Talk to Santa" instead found they had called the operations hotline of the Director of Operations of CONAD (the Continental Air Defense Command). Buried deep under Cheyenne Mountain in Wyoming, this was the government's defence arm charged with giving America early radar warning of attack from missiles or planes.

Colonel Harry Shoup was astonished to be listening to a six-year-old boy reading through his Christmas wish list. After several such calls, he ordered his

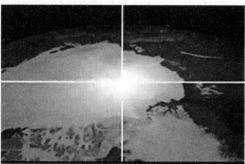

staff to tell the young callers that CONAD was giving Santa Claus a helping hand and that its radars were already picking him up heading towards America from the North Pole. The story got into the press, so perhaps CONAD shouldn't have been too surprised when they were inundated with calls the following year from kids wanting to know where Santa was. A tradition had begun.

For more than half a century now CONAD, and its replacement NORAD (North American Air Defense Command, a joint operation with Canada), have 'tracked'

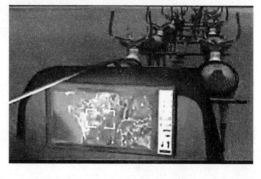

Santa each year. Since 1989, children not just in North America, but anywhere in the world, have been able to log on to *www.noradsanta.org* on Christmas Eve in one of six languages and follow the big red guy's progress across the globe. Across Canada and Alaska 47 radar sites check for indications of Santa leaving the North Pole. When they have confirmation of lift-off, geo-synchronous satellites orbiting 22,300 miles above the Earth apparently home in on the infrared signature

given off by Rudolph's nose (or so the NORAD website has it).

Since the advent of the website, which goes live each November, an array of high-speed digital Santa Cams around the world tracks Santa as he delivers the presents, producing still and moving images. In much the same way that movie aliens have a predilection for raining down destruction on well-known buildings, so NORAD's Santa Cams only ever seem to spot the great man as he's passing tourist spots such as the Taj Mahal, Buckingham Palace or the Statue of Liberty.

As Santa enters North American airspace, NORAD's fighter pilots (Canadian CF-18s and American F-15s or F-16s) are scrambled to intercept him and escort him on the last leg of his delivery route, ending up in Hawaii. In 2004, the website got 912 million hits. There were also 55,000 phone calls. If you want to call NORAD, the number's 001-877-446-6723, though it's always possible they've retaliated by giving out Sears Roebuck's number.

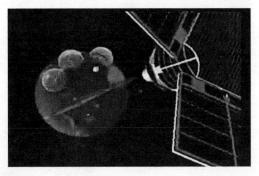

Given the publicity that NORAD's annual Santa tracking gets, it's a wonder that during the Cold War, the Russians didn't try to get a missile through disguised as a sleigh and reindeer.

Pull the other one

The world's largest functional Christmas cracker was 181ft long and nearly 12ft high. It was made in Sydney, Australia in 1998, and was pulled at a shopping centre there on December 16th. There's no record of how many people it took to pull it – or, more importantly, how naff the trinket that fell out was.

I wish it could be Christmas every day

Andy Park is addicted to Christmas. How else can you describe someone who has celebrated Christmas every single day for nigh on 13 years? The 46-year-old electrician breakfasts each day on six mince pies, a turkey sandwich, Christmas pudding, cream and a glass of sherry. He then rushes through his work, knocking off at 11.30 so he can cook his roast turkey lunch ready to sit down at 2pm. At 3pm he watches a recording of the Queen's speech, sherry glass in hand. Then he invites in neighbours, friends, relatives – even people passing the house – to pull crackers and let off party poppers.

It all began when Andy was feeling depressed one day, and decided that the only thing that would cheer him up would be a Christmas dinner. He enjoyed it so much, he decided to make it a daily event.

Andy's obsession has so far cost him over £250,000 and has seen him consume vast quantities of Christmas fare (see facing page). Each night he wraps a couple of presents for himself to open the following day.

Understandably perhaps, Andy – who lives in the West Country – is divorced, though he has a girlfriend who, like his daughter, thinks he's a 'crackpot'. If he goes to a restaurant or a friend's house, or even abroad, he insists on a full Christmas dinner. "If they don't cook it, I won't go," he told us.

Five years ago, his doctor warned him that Christmas could kill him, as his weight had almost doubled to 21 stone. Instead of going cold turkey, however,

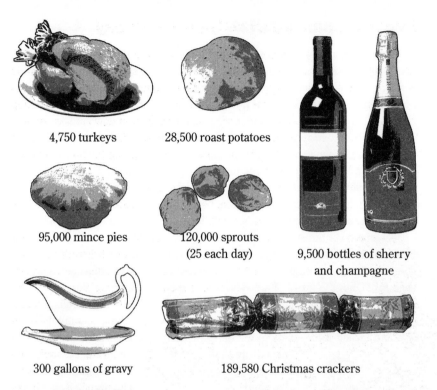

4,750 turkeys   28,500 roast potatoes

95,000 mince pies   120,000 sprouts
(25 each day)

9,500 bottles of sherry
and champagne

300 gallons of gravy   189,580 Christmas crackers

Above: Andy Park's Christmas fare consumption to date. In addition, he has also got through 36 ovens and 42 video recorders.

Andy got a dog to walk and joined a gym, which brought his weight back down to a mere 15-and-a-half stone.

For Christmas 2005, Andy released a single called *It's Christmas Every Day*. Sadly, it didn't set the charts alight but went the way of his previous records, *The Christmas Man*, *Yuletime Oh Yeah* and *Alleluia It's Christmas*. Andy continues to invite celebrities to his house for an unseasonal Christmas lunch, and dozens of household names have graced his dinner table – including Ruby Wax, Tessa Sanderson and Cliff Richard.

His big ambition, apart from singing with Des O'Connor, is to have the Queen deliver her Christmas message from his front room. We can't understand why she keeps turning him down.

How does Santa do it?

In 1990 *Spy* magazine published a 'scientific' study on Santa. With 300,000 animal species still to be classified, they didn't rule out the possibility of flying reindeer. However, their calculations about Santa's big night weren't so encouraging.

Excluding those religions that don't go in for Christmas, they calculated that Santa had to deliver presents to 378 million children in 91.8 million homes. Travelling east to west, he would have 31 hours to do his work.

Santa would have a mere 1/1000 of a second to stop at each home, shin down the chimney, fill the stockings, eat the mince pie, shimmy back up the chimney and get the sleigh moving to the next home. He'd have to cover 75.5 million miles at an average speed of 650 miles a second – 3,000 times the speed of sound.

Taking the average present to be a 1 kilo Lego set, the sleigh's payload would be 350,000 tons – four times the weight of the QE2. Travelling at 650 miles per second, the air resistance would cause the lead reindeers to absorb 14.3 quintillion Joules of energy. They'd instantly burst into flame and cause horrendous sonic booms while Santa, not the fittest of individuals, would be subjected to 17,500 times the force of gravity, pinning him to the seat with a force of 4.3 million pounds.

The world's scientists instantly gave up searching for cold fusion and their car keys and turned their minds to the Santa problem. Dr Arnold Pompos of high-

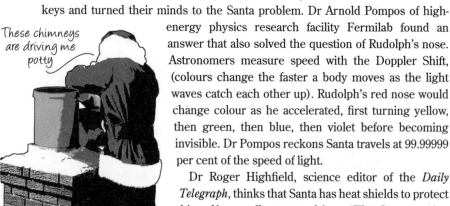

These chimneys are driving me potty

energy physics research facility Fermilab found an answer that also solved the question of Rudolph's nose. Astronomers measure speed with the Doppler Shift, (colours change the faster a body moves as the light waves catch each other up). Rudolph's red nose would change colour as he accelerated, first turning yellow, then green, then blue, then violet before becoming invisible. Dr Pompos reckons Santa travels at 99.99999 per cent of the speed of light.

Dr Roger Highfield, science editor of the *Daily Telegraph*, thinks that Santa has heat shields to protect himself, as well as warp drives. "The *Spy* magazine allegation is outrageous," he said. "We know Santa delivers those presents on Christmas Eve as reliably as we know Rudolph's nose is red."

And then, presumably, yellow, green, blue, violet and invisible.

Born on Christmas Day

1583	Orlando Gibbons, composer	1918	Anwar Sadat, president
1642	Isaac Newton, mathematician	1924	Rod Serling, writer
1771	Dorothy Wordsworth, diarist	1935	Little Richard, singer
1887	Conrad Hilton, hotel magnate	1944	Kenny Everett, comedian
1893	Robert Ripley, trivialist	1946	Jimmy Buffett, singer
1899	Humphrey Bogart, actor	1949	Sissy Spacek, actress
1906	Lew Grade, film & TV producer	1954	Annie Lennox, singer
1907	Cab Calloway, band leader	1957	Shane McGowan, singer
1908	Quentin Crisp, author	1971	Dido, singer
1914	Tony Martin, singer	1975	Marcus Trescothick, cricketer

Died on Christmas Day

1826	Yoshohito, emperor of Japan	1983	Joan Miro, painter
1938	Karel Capek, Czech author	1989	Nicolae Ceausescu, dictator
1946	W C Fields, actor	1995	Dean Martin, singer
1977	Charlie Chaplin, actor	2000	W V O Quine, philosopher
1979	Joan Blondell, actor	2005	Birgit Nilsson, soprano

Also on Christmas Day

800	Coronation of Charlemagne as Holy Roman Emperor
1066	Coronation of William the Conqueror
1223	St Francis of Assisi invents nativity scene
1776	George Washington crosses the Delaware
1952	Queen makes first Christmas broadcast
1991	Mikhail Gorbachev resigns as leader of Soviet Union
2003	Mars space probe *Beagle 2* disappears

Christmas number one hits in the UK

The singles charts were recorded from 1952. For earlier dates, positions are based on sheet music sales. Not included here is the best-selling Christmas record of all time – Bing Crosby's 1942 hit *White Christmas*.

1945	Issy Bonn	I'm In Love With Two Sweethearts
1946	Frank Sinatra	Five Minutes More
1947	Lou Preager & Jimmy Leach	An Apple Blossom Wedding
1948	Dinah Shore & Evelyn Knight	Buttons And Bows
1949	Anton Karas	The Harry Lime Theme
1950	Gene Autry & Bing Crosby	Rudolph The Red-Nosed Reindeer
1951	Teddy Johnson & Teresa Brewer	Longing For You
1952	Al Martino	Here In My Heart
1953	Frankie Laine	Answer Me
1954	Winifred Atwell	Let's Have Another Party
1955	Dickie Valentine	Christmas Alphabet
1956	Johnnie Ray	Just Walkin' In The Rain
1957	Harry Belafonte	Mary's Boy Child
1958	Conway Twitty	It's Only Make Believe
1959	Emile Ford & The Checkmates	What Do You Want To Make Those Eyes At Me For
1960	Cliff Richard & The Shadows	I Love You
1961	Danny Williams	Moon River
1962	Elvis Presley	Return To Sender
1963	The Beatles	I Want To Hold Your Hand
1964	The Beatles	I Feel Fine
1965	The Beatles	Day Tripper / We Can Work It Out
1966	Tom Jones	The Green Grass Of Home
1967	The Beatles	Hello Goodbye
1968	Scaffold	Lily The Pink
1969	Rolf Harris	Two Little Boys
1970	Dave Edmunds	I Hear You Knockin'
1971	Benny Hill	Ernie (Fastest Milkman In The West)
1972	Little Jimmy Osmond	Long Haired Lover From Liverpool
1973	Slade	Merry Xmas Everybody
1974	Mud	Lonely This Christmas
1975	Queen	Bohemian Rhapsody

1976	Johnny Mathis	When A Child Is Born (Soleado)
1977	Wings	Mull Of Kintyre
1978	Boney M	Mary's Boy Child
1979	Pink Floyd	Another Brick In The Wall
1980	St Winifred's School Choir	There's No One Quite Like Grandma
1981	The Human League	Don't You Want Me
1982	Renee & Renato	Save Your Love
1983	The Flying Pickets	Only You
1984	Band Aid	Do They Know It's Christmas?
1985	Shakin' Stevens	Merry Christmas Everyone
1986	Jackie Wilson	Reet Petite
1987	The Pet Shop Boys	Always On My Mind
1988	Cliff Richard	Mistletoe & Wine
1989	Band Aid II	Do They Know It's Christmas?
1990	Cliff Richard	Saviour's Day
1991	Queen	Bohemian Rhapsody
1992	Whitney Houston	I Will Always Love You
1993	Mr Blobby	Mr Blobby
1994	East 17	Stay Another Day
1995	Michael Jackson	Earth Song
1996	Spice Girls	2 Become 1
1997	Spice Girls	Too Much
1998	Spice Girls	Goodbye
1999	Westlife	I Have A Dream / Seasons In The Sun
2000	Bob The Builder	Can We Fix It?
2001	Robbie Williams & Nicole Kidman	Somethin' Stupid
2002	Girls Aloud	Sound Of The Underground
2003	Michael Andrews & Gary Jules	Mad World
2004	Band Aid 20	Do They Know It's Christmas?
2005	Shayne Ward	That's My Goal

I'm only hiding because I'm a little elf conscious

In a recent poll, the 1988 Cliff Richard song *Mistletoe & Wine* topped the list of the most dreaded Christmas songs of all time. The 'bottom ten' list included Johnny Mathis' *When A Child Is Born*, Wham's *Last Christmas*, Slade's *Merry Christmas Everybody* and Wizzard's *I Wish It Could Be Christmas Every Day*. You'll be able to hear them in any supermarket from mid-October.

This seems like a good place for a quiet snooze

A cracking tale

Among the list of great inventors – Edison, Curie, Whittle, Brunel, Baird – one name is always missing, that of Tom Smith. Where is his blue plaque? Where was his knighthood? For Tom Smith was none other than the inventor of that great British tradition, the Christmas cracker.

In the mid-19th century, Smith – a manufacturer of sweets – was on holiday in France. There, he discovered bon-bons, sugared almonds sold in twists of waxed paper. Back home, he produced some just in time for Christmas and they were a big hit.

By the following Christmas, rivals were copying him, so Smith added love mottos. Another roaring success. But it wasn't long before his competitors were aping him again.

His next move was to add a little trinket in a tube as well as the sweet and the motto. These were sold as 'Christmas Bonbonnes', but Smith still felt something was lacking. Inspiration struck sitting in front of the fire. A log suddenly crackled loudly and Tom Smith had his epiphany. It was two years later – 1860 – before he had perfected and was able to sell his 'Bangs of Expectation'. These contained two pieces of thin card pasted with a little saltpetre that rubbed together to make a bang as the cracker was pulled. Known initially as 'Cosaques' because the noise was thought to resemble the whips of Cossacks, it took a generation before the name mutated into 'crackers'.

Rivals were still hot on Smith's heels and, in these early days, crackers were said sometimes to catch light when pulled. They were incredibly varied and impressive compared to today's version, with Shakespeare-themed crackers containing quotations and even hats from the plays, model cottages and landscapes, games and toys that could be constructed with parts from all the crackers in the set and even stereoscopic crackers containing kaleidoscopes.

The main day for Victorian cracker-pulling was Twelfth Night, a period of rowdy and often extremely mischievous celebrations. Queen Victoria apparently wasn't amused and tried to have this un-Christian festival suppressed.

By the end of the 19th century, Smith's factory was turning out 13 million crackers a year. The gifts, like the crackers, would be made by hand: glass pendants, bracelets, brooches and other jewellery from Bohemia, paper fans from the Orient, ivory elephants from India, musical toys from the Continent. A set in the 1860s called 'Star Cosaques' contained bottles of French perfume.

During World War II Tom Smith's firm received an order from the Ministry of Defence for bundles of snaps – the strips inside the crackers that make the noise – with string attached, to imitate the noise of machine guns for training soldiers.

In Finsbury Square in the City of London is a drinking fountain erected by Walter Smith in memory of his mother, Mary, and father, Tom, inventor of the great British cracker.

How to pull a cracker

It's a little hard to believe but scientists at the University of Surrey really have studied the best way of pulling a Christmas cracker. According to physicist Dr Paul Stevenson, "the answer is simple":

$$p = \frac{s \times (10 - j) \times (10 - t)}{81 \times (A + 1)} \times \frac{n_y}{(n_y + n_o)}$$

…where p is the 'probability' of winning, j the 'jerk' ratio – how strongly you're pulling compared to your opponent – t the 'twist factor', n_y and n_o the 'number of times' you and your opponent have respectively won previous cracker pulls, s the 'stare factor' and, perhaps most importantly of all, A is the number of 'units of alcohol' you have drunk in excess of your opponent.

What this means, according to Dr Stevenson, is that you should "let the opponent do most of the work, twisting and weakening the bonds at his end of the cracker – whilst your pull remains straight."

Now all they need to tell us is *why* anyone would be bothered about who wins when you pull a cracker.

A timeline of popular toys

6000 BC An Indian game, *Chaturanga*, becomes chess

4000 BC Babylonians invent checkers

3000 BC First backgammon set appears in Samaria

1000 BC Kites make their first appearance in China

969 AD The first playing cards are seen in Asia

1759 Joseph Merlin invents roller-skates

1867 Indian *Parcheesi* is marketed as *Ludo*

1884 Brothers Ivarson from Osby make *Brio* trains

1886 Parents shocked by the invention of the child's BB gun

1880s The Chinese invent *Mah Jongg*

1900 Joshua Lionel Cowen invents first battery train set

1902 Teddy bears named after Teddy Roosevelt

1903 Binney & Smith make first *Crayola* crayons

1931 One-time architect Alfred Butts invents *Scrabble*

1932 Ole Christiansen invents *Lego*

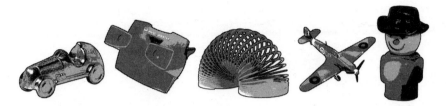

1934 Charles Darrow devises *Monopoly*

1939 Piano tuner invents *ViewMaster*

1943 Navy engineer invents *Slinky*

1948 Airfix makes first plastic kit

1950 Fisher Price introduce *Little People*

1952 Hasbro introduce *Mr Potato Head*

1952 *Pez* mint dispenser is launched

1952 Jack Odell makes the *Matchbox* car

1956 First *Play-Doh* sold as wallpaper cleaner

1957 Group of teachers invent the *Tonka* truck

1957 Frisbee Baking Co. pie tin becomes *Frisbee*

1959 Elliot and Ruth Handler invent *Barbie*

1965 Hasbro introduce *Spirograph* and *Twister*

1971 Hans Beck creates first *Playmobil* characters

1972 Magnavox invents the video game, and the rot sets in

Toys of the year

On the previous page we looked at the history of toys through the ages. Here, bringing us bang up to date, is the definitive list of the best UK toys of the past 40 years, as selected by the Toy Retailers Association. Excuse us while we wipe a nostalgic tear from our eyes...

1965	James Bond Aston Martin
1966	Action Man
1967	Spirograph
1968	Sindy
1969	Hot Wheels cars
1970	Sindy
1971	Katie Kopykat writing doll
1972	Plasticraft modelling kits

1973	Mastermind board game
1974	Lego Family set
1975	Lego Basic set
1976	Peter Powell kites
1977	Playmobil Playpeople
1978	Britains Combine Harvester
1979	Legoland Space kits
1980 1981	Rubik's Cube

1982 1983	Star Wars toys
1984	Masters of the Universe
1985 1986	Transformers

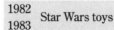

1987	
1988	Sylvanian Families
1989	
1990	Teenage Mutant Ninja Turtles
1991	Nintendo Gameboy
1992	WWF Wrestlers
1993	Thunderbirds Tracey Island
1994	Power Rangers
1995	POGS
1996	Barbie
1997	Teletubbies
1998	Furby
1999	Furby Babies
2000	Teksta
2001	Bionicles
2002 2003	Beyblades
2004	Robosapien
2005	Tamagotchi

6 Fun and games

CHRISTMAS IS A TIME when we're forced to spend hours in the company of near-strangers. Our families, that is.

Both during the sherry-fuelled warm-up period before lunch, and in the bloated stretch of motionlessness that follows a traditional blow-out, we need a way to relieve the tension and prevent those old family arguments from resurfacing.

Here's a collection of our favourite games and pastimes. You'll find a scintillating selection of both physical and mental activities – some old, some you won't have seen before – ranging from the cerebral to the downright silly. We've also provided some handy tips on how to succeed at those old seasonal favourites, *Monopoly, Cluedo, Trivial Pursuit* and *Scrabble*.

Because Christmas is a period of enforced enjoyment, we've thrown in a few pages of jokey nonsense that has no purpose other than to keep you entertained – including two very different takes on the Twelve Days of Christmas.

And if all that isn't enough, we've included a page of jokes so lamentable we were ashamed even to put them in our crackers.

Getting in touch with Santa

In the far-off days before email, the only way you could send Santa your Christmas wish list was to write it on a piece of paper, and burn it in the grate so its message went up the chimney. This is still a great way to find out what your children really want – but remember to read the list before consigning it to the flames, or you'll need all your forensic skills to decipher the ashes.

These days, you can write to Father Christmas at Reindeerland, SAN TA1. There are also plenty of websites where you can talk to him directly – and stop off to buy Christmas merchandise while you're there. The internet has brought a new meaning to the commercialisation of the Christmas message.

Our favourite site is *www.emailsanta.com*, which will give you a personalised reply from ol' whitebeard in seconds. We wondered, though: does Santa really take the time to peruse each message he receives? Or is there, perhaps, the suggestion that he doesn't take quite enough time off from toymaking and sack-stuffing to give his responses the consideration they deserve?

We sent the following message to the site, using their standard automated form, to see what sort of reply we'd get. As we suspected, Santa was perhaps too busy that day to really take in the content of our missive.

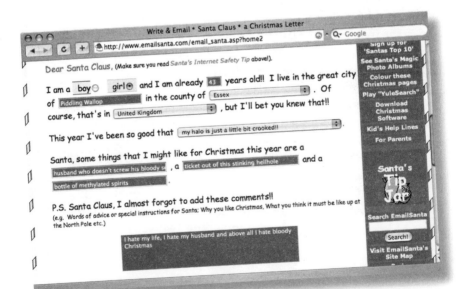

#1, Rudolph Way
Reindeerland, North Pole
SAN TA1

Piddling Wallop, Essex
United Kingdom

Thursday, March 23, 2006

HO!! Ho!! ho!! Suicidal Margaret!!

Thank you for sending me your email all the way from Piddling Wallop! Did you know that Piddling Wallop is one of Mrs. Claus' favourite places? The other thing she really likes is to read all your wonderful emails. As a matter of fact, she was just asking if I had heard from you lately!

My goodness, Suicidal Margaret! Are you fibbing to ol' Santa Claus?!? You can't possibly be 43 years old already! Why it seems like only yesterday that I was leaving presents for a certain little girl and here you are now, practically one of Santa's elves! (*grin*)

Sorry the presents the last little while probably haven't been quite as exciting as they were when you were a little girl but, well, you know how these things go (*wink*). Anyway, Santa's glad to see some of the 'older kids' (not to mention anyone in particular!) still take the time to write. I also hear you've been a really good girl. (Of course, you won't mind if I do a little checking, will you? HO!! Ho!! ho!!).

Let's see what you put in your letter for Christmas wishes: 1. a husband who doesn't screw his bloody secretary; 2. a ticket out of this stinking hell hole and; 3. a bottle of methylated spirits. HO!! Ho!! ho!! Those ARE good presents Suicidal Margaret! The elves have been working very hard, but its been such a busy year that I hope you won't be too upset with me if you don't get everything you wished for.

HO!! Ho!! ho!! Rudolph wants to take me for another test ride in the sleigh so I better get going! The new sleigh is 'Internet-equipped' so I can even send & receive emails Christmas Eve! I hope you'll come back to EmailSanta.com Christmas Eve to watch me go around the world! Take care Suicidal Margaret and don't forget to come back and visit me here at EmailSanta.com on Christmas Eve!! And remember... only 277 more sleeps until Christmas!!

Love You Forever and Always,

Father Christmas

The 12 emails of Christmas

From: Melissa Newby
To: James Truelove
Date: 25 Dec 2006 11:04 am

Darling James,

What a fantastic present! I just love the pear tree, and look forward to the day when it bears fruit. You are such a sweetie!

Your ever-loving

Melissa

PS The partridge was delicious, many thanks.

———

From: Melissa Newby
To: James Truelove
Date: 26 Dec 2006 10:36 am

Dearest James,

Lucky I'm not prone to putting on weight! My mother came round unexpectedly, so that brace of pigeons turned out to be just the ticket. Where ever did you find white ones???

You are so kind.

Melissa

———

From: Melissa Newby
To: James Truelove
Date: 27 Dec 2006 10:47 am

Dear James,

Your concern for my wellbeing is admirable! And I really do appreciate the chickens. The trouble is there really isn't room in the freezer for all three of them, so I've given two to the homeless shelter. Hope you don't mind.

You really must stop sending me poultry!

Lots of love

Melissa

———

From: Melissa Newby
To: James Truelove
Date: 28 Dec 2006 12:44 pm

Dear James,

Is one of your mates a poacher? Tell them to get something with more meat on next time!

There's barely enough on those birds to make them worth the bother.

Love

Melissa

———

From: Melissa Newby
To: James Truelove
Date: 29 Dec 2006 9:04 am

My wonderful, darling Jimmy,

One gold ring is beautiful – but five!!!! One for each finger, I suppose. Is this a proposal of marriage? I'm not sure having them delivered by Argos is quite the same as going down on bended knee, but consider yourself accepted!

Yours for ever and ever,

Melissa

———

From: Melissa Newby
To: James Truelove
Date: 30 Dec 2006 2:14 pm

Darling Jimbo,

Do you expect we're going to live on a farm when we're married? Six geese! Really, darling, I don't know where we're going to put the things. I hope you love omelettes, they won't stop laying eggs!

Yours always,

Melissa

———

From: Melissa Newby
To: James Truelove
Date: 31 Dec 2006 11:48 am

Dearest Jimmy,

I really don't know what I'm going to do with seven swans. Apart from fighting with the geese, they do make such a mess. Please arrange for someone to come round and collect them straight away. I have better things to do than clean up swan poop!

Please stop now, dearest, it's getting silly.

Melissa

From: Melissa Newby
To: James Truelove
Date: 1 Jan 2007 6:47 am

Dear James,

Happy new year? I don't think so. Woken up at 6am (with a blinding headache) by eight milkmaids at the door, who said you'd sent them. They weren't at all pleased when I told them I didn't have a cow. By the time I'd given them all a cup of tea and sent them home I was feeling really quite shattered.

This really has gone far enough.

Yours

Melissa

From: Melissa Newby
To: James Truelove
Date: 2 Jan 2007 2:18 pm

Dear James,

How on earth do you expect me to explain away nine dancing girls to the neighbours? I'm surprised you know such 'ladies'. This sort of thing may be all very well on a stag night, but frankly I'm a little put out to think that you'd imagine I'd be pleased. If this is the sort of company you keep, I may have to rethink our wedding plans.

Yours

Melissa

From: Melissa Newby
To: James Truelove
Date: 3 Jan 2007 10:55 am

James,

Being assaulted in my own home by ten drunken aristocrats really is the last straw. Have you ANY idea what they and the dancing girls are up to right now? I'm sorry, James, but we must consider our engagement at an end.

Best wishes

Melissa

From: Melissa Newby
To: James Truelove
Date: 4 Jan 2007 7:29 am

James, you bastard, I really think you're taking the rejection thing too hard – waking me up in the middle of the night with the Glasgow Bagpipe Band, or whoever those awful people were. It shows just what a mean-spirited, small-minded man you really are.

Leave me alone, James, and please don't bother me any more.

Melissa

From: A J P Wetherspoon
To: James Truelove Esq
Date: 5 Jan 2007 11:19 am

Dear Sir,

We have been instructed by our client, Ms Melissa Newby, to issue a Cease and Desist order upon you forthwith. You are hereby directed to affirm that you will not attempt to effect contact, in person or by proxy, with Ms Newby from this date forth.

In addition, we understand from the local constabulary that proceedings are to be taken against you regarding a breach of the peace incident involving a number of percussionists in your employ.

We trust we shall have no cause to pursue this matter further.

Yours faithfully

Arthur Wetherspoon
Stanhope & Wetherspoon
Solicitors

Christmas present games

You may think giving presents is enough of an activity in itself – and you may well be right. But here are a few ideas that may add a little spice to the occasion.

Wrap-up

Keeping the kids occupied in the run-up to Christmas can be tricky. Despite their enthusiasm for receiving presents, it doesn't always extend to the hard work of giving them, namely wrapping them up. To make it harder – and keep them busy for longer – get them to wrap presents in pairs, handicapped by either holding hands or keeping one hand behind their back.

It isn't the easiest task in the world, so the chances are you're going to have to rewrap them later, unless you can give Aunt Lucy her present during one of her "Where *are* my glasses?" moments. But at least it will keep the little darlings out of your way while you get on with the *real* business of wrapping.

Can I come out now?

Getting warmer

Children tend to be overwhelmed by a multitude of presents on Christmas Day. To save the frenzy of a concentrated bout of gluttonous unwrapping, we recommend hiding presents around the room – under cushions, in cupboards, under the bed, behind the curtains. You can call out "getting warmer" as they approach a hidden gift, and "getting colder" when they're far away from one. Build up to "getting really warm now", all the way up to "boiling hot!" when they're standing right on top of it and haven't noticed. It's a great way to spin the fun out that much longer!

Secret Santa

This is a Christmas custom familiar to anyone who works in an office. Each person is given a budget of, say, £5 or £10, and has to buy a gift for another person in the office. There are two methods: either you buy an anonymous present for someone whose name has been picked from a hat for you, or you just buy a general present and they're given out in a random way.

A few pointers: don't overspend; you have a budget, so stick to it. Naturally, human nature being what it is, many people try to find the most embarrassing presents for their colleagues.

Above all, remember to look delighted when you open your own present, even though it won't be anywhere near as well-chosen or as tastefully wrapped as the gift *you* donated.

This was a real bargain!

Secret Santa's revenge

This curious variation is becoming popular in American workplaces, where it's more commonly known as the White Elephant Gift Exchange. While it seems to us that it's more likely to cause bad feeling than seasonal cheer, it's an interesting alternative to the standard British version.

Here's how it works: each person buys a present of the agreed value, and wraps it up. Everyone then draws lots to set the order in which they will take part. The first person then takes any gift they like the look of, and opens it. The second person can then choose whether to pick any unwrapped gift from the pile, or may opt to 'steal' the already opened gift belonging to the first person. If they do so, the first person can choose another gift to replace it.

Play continues in a similar fashion, with each person choosing any gift they like – either one that's already been opened (and is now in the possession of someone else) or one from the wrapped pile. As before, if your gift is stolen, you can then steal someone else's.

To prevent things getting totally out of hand, there are a couple of additional rules: first, that a gift can only be stolen once during a turn; and second, that if a gift has had three owners, then the third owner gets to keep it permanently.

After the last person has had their go, the first person – who didn't get the chance to do this at the beginning – can then steal someone else's, starting another round of exchanges until everyone is happy. Or feeling miserable, cheated and deprived, as the case may be.

Party games

The whole family doesn't *have* to slump in front of the telly simply because there's an unexpected lull in the food supply. You can always play a few games, and it isn't essential to pay a small fortune for a new board game that consists of little more than some roughly moulded plastic counters and an instruction manual poorly translated from the original Taiwanese.

Here are a few games that are as fun to watch as they are to participate in, and which can be played with just a few household objects. There are no complicated rules to master, either.

Stringing them along

We all know that game involving passing an orange along a row of people without using your hands. It was pretty sexy and funny when Cary Grant and Audrey Hepburn did it in *Charade,* but you might not want to get quite so cosy with all

your relations. Instead, try the String and Spoon Race. You need two wooden spoons with either a hole in the handle, or a deep notch around the end to which you can attach a long length of string.

Divide into two teams, lined up next to each other. Each player in turn must push the spoon (with the string) down one arm of their clothing and down one leg, then pass the spoon to the player behind them. Depending on numbers and time, either finish when the first spoon has reached the back of the line, or else make the players return it to the front, with the first player winding the string back up into a ball.

Players have to go through extraordinary contortions, particularly if wearing tight trousers which have been placed under even greater strain by several days of overindulgence. Providing the first person hangs onto the end of the string, the whole line may end up with flailing limbs, like a line of puppets gone mad. If your party includes a maiden aunt or two, you can always restrict the spoon's journey to the upper half of the body.

Balloonatics

Stuffy Uncle Fred will have trouble maintaining that annoying superior air if you rope him into this game. It's a little like necking the orange but, instead of oranges and necks, two teams must pass those long balloons along the line without using their hands. As the balloons are passed back from one set of knees to the next, it proves pretty tricky not to give them a helping hand. Any hands, any dropped balloons or any bangs, and that team has to start again.

Pop goes the weasel

Ailing grandparents might want to sit this one out, particularly if they're a martyr to their gout (does anyone actually *get* gout nowadays?).

Round balloons, each blown up to the same size, are tied to one ankle of each player. The aim is to burst the other players' balloons without yours getting popped. Naturally, no hands may be used.

Balloon football

Each player should have a regular balloon and one of those long, sausage-like ones. The simple aim is to use the long one as a bat to hit the other balloon into a cardboard box placed a few feet away – it's an awful lot harder than it sounds. A

gloriously silly game, but one that's unlikely to do long-term damage to the furniture.

Unless you relish arguments along the lines of "That's mine", "No, it's not", you should ensure that the round balloons are all different colours.

The devil's tongue race

What *do* you call those things that squawk and unroll when you blow them? Party blowers? Some know them as 'devil's tongues'. Whatever your favourite name for them, you can have a great race using them to push empty matchboxes along the ground. If you haven't much space, set up a competition with heats culminating in a grand final.

If you don't have blowers or matchboxes, but can lay your hands on some Ping Pong balls, you can do something similar getting players to push them around a course with their noses. It's funniest if the course has at least one sharp turn in it. If you don't want a head-to-head race, set up a time trial instead, with the fastest time around the track winning.

Pick up the packet

Hang on to empty cereal packets in December so you can play this simple game. A packet, with the top torn off, is placed on the ground. Everyone then tries to bend over and pick it up with just their teeth (no hands allowed and certainly no kneeling down).

After one round, anyone who hasn't managed it is out, a strip is torn off the top of the box and around you go again. Lower and lower the box gets until finally, there is only one person who can pick it up.

The game has a big advantage for family gatherings in that unfit adults are at a distinct disadvantage to more limber (and shorter) children.

Oi! I live there!

Celebhead

Prepare a stack of small Post-It Notes, writing on each the name of somebody famous, fictional or real, contemporary or historic. As your guests arrive, stick one of these to their foreheads without them seeing the name, pressing it all over to make sure it will stay on. Instruct them to talk to other partygoers as if they are the celebrity mentioned on their Post-It Note.

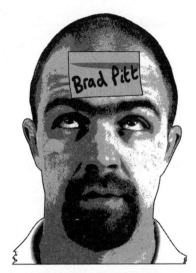

It's a great icebreaker as people try to guess their 'own' identity. Ideally, people should work out who they are from the way other guests behave with them; but if they get stuck, they can always ask a few pertinent (or even impertinent) questions. It also works well at the table if there's an unscheduled pause between courses.

If everyone knows each other well at a party, you can try replacing the names of celebrities with those of the partygoers. One or two people could even have their own name on their forehead. Can you recognise yourself from the way other people see you?

How's yours?

One person leaves the room, while the others decide on a familiar object. This could be a toenail, a nose, a car, a bed – anything, as long as it applies to everyone in the room. It could even be something more abstract, like a mortgage or their last holiday, or the view from their bedroom window.

When the person outside returns, they have to guess what the thing is by asking each player in turn, "How's yours?" The players then have to respond with an adjective to describe their object. So a car might be described as "purple" or "scratched" or even "non-existent".

The clever part comes from thinking up descriptions that don't give the game away too early. So while describing your car as "speedy" or "unleaded" would be too obvious, words like "taxing" or "thirsty" will help to spin it out a bit longer. Ambiguity is the key to making this game work – and inventive answers will extend the fun.

Charades

Everybody knows how to play Charades. Unfortunately, not everyone knows the same rules. In the interests of holiday harmony, here's our preferred version of one of the great games for a large group.

Making sure that the teams are evenly split, dribbling babies matched with dribbling grannies, one person must act out silently something chosen by the other team. Rather than have to come up with clues on the spur of the moment, you can always get people to write down suggestions earlier. As it's a family gathering, not *University Challenge*, don't make the charades too difficult.

Most importantly, the person acting out the charade must make no noise at all. They should indicate whether the charade to be guessed is a play (curtains parting), a film (a hand-cranked movie camera), a TV show (mime a box shape), a song (mime singing), a book (mime opening a book) or even a phrase or quote (making quotation marks in the air).

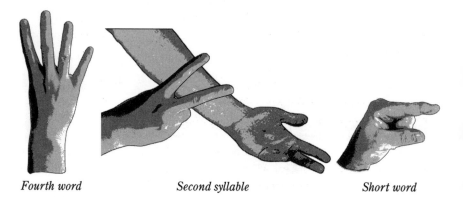

Fourth word   *Second syllable*   *Short word*

The mimer indicates the number of words in the charade and then holds up their fingers again, showing which of the words they are about to act out. The number of syllables is indicated by placing that number of fingers on the forearm, followed by an indication for the syllable they're expecting people to guess.

If the entire phrase is to be acted out, a grand sweeping motion will indicate this. Other generally accepted gestures including holding up a thumb and finger close together to indicate a short word ("a", "the" etc), bringing hands together to indicate the guessers should shorten the word or moving them apart if the word needs to be longer. Also useful is to touch your ear if you want to act out a word that sounds like another. If someone gets it right, touch your nose and then point to them, pointing without a nose-touch if they are the closest.

Ingenuity always pays off. For example, you could act out the word 'God' by getting down on all fours, behaving like a dog and walking backwards. We have a rule that you should to try to act out the whole thing first, before breaking it down into individual words – which is great fun to watch, especially if the subject is a complicated film or book.

If experience teaches you that playing with teams leads to something akin to civil war, why not have each mimer act out a charade of their own devising to the entire gathering?

Christmas with the Wright family

This is a game that can even be played at the table to keep some semblance of order if the next course is taking a while arriving. It requires a number of wrapped presents, either brought by guests or prepared in advance by the hosts.

During the story, everyone must pass a gift to their left or right, whenever they hear the relevant word uttered. At the end of the tale, everyone can open the present in front of them.

It was Christmas Eve in the WRIGHT household, and Mother WRIGHT was LEFT at home while the other WRIGHTS, Father WRIGHT, Lizzie WRIGHT and Ronnie WRIGHT, did some last-minute shopping. They had LEFT a couple of hours ago and RIGHT at that moment, they returned.

In marched the other WRIGHTS, Father WRIGHT barking out steps, LEFT, RIGHT, LEFT, RIGHT to Lizzie WRIGHT and Ronnie WRIGHT. Father WRIGHT was holding a package the postman had LEFT by the front door. "Who LEFT that?" asked Mother WRIGHT. "It's from Grandpa WRIGHT," said Father WRIGHT.

"Grandpa's a RIGHT meanie," said Ronnie WRIGHT.

"Don't talk like that," said Mother WRIGHT. "It isn't RIGHT. Grandpa LEFT last year in a bad mood. You must be nice to him this year and WRITE a thank you letter later. RIGHT?"

"RIGHT!" groaned Lizzie WRIGHT and Ronnie WRIGHT. But if it were LEFT to them, they wouldn't WRITE any thank you letters at all.

"Oh no," said Father WRIGHT, counting the shopping bags. "We've LEFT some of the shopping at the supermarket. We'll have to go RIGHT back there and start all over again."

Consequences

A remarkably common game a generation ago, Consequences is sadly almost forgotten now. Depending on the complexion of the gathering, it can be innocuous or rather more cheeky. Everyone is given a piece of paper and writes a male name at the top (famous, fictional or family), folding the paper over to hide the name before passing the paper to the next person.

They should write down a female name before folding and passing the paper on. Next should be written where they met, then what he said, then what she said, rounding off with the consequence.

With the words "met", "at", "he said", "she said" and "and the consequence was" inserted in between what's written on the paper, you end up with vaguely surreal, often silly, tales along the lines of, "The Prince of Wales met Wonder Woman at Sainsbury's. He said, 'I've got a pimple on my bottom.' She said, 'It's purple, isn't it?' And the consequence was that they both emigrated to live together on a remote desert island."

A more sophisticated version of Consequences is Mad Libs, invented in the 1950s by a pair of American comedy writers. They're essentially stories with blank holes. Players are asked to put down words such as a noun, a person's name, an adjective, a colour and so on. The story is then read out with the substituted words. Not only are Mad Libs often hysterical, but they're also very useful for helping children get to grips with nouns, adjectives, plurals and so on.

If you don't have any Mad Libs books to hand, you can find plenty online or even invent your own; early reading books can be adapted perfectly.

Paper Telephone

We've seen this game called Fax Machine, Cricket Cricket and even Eat Poop You Cat. But we think Paper Telephone is a good word for it.

It's akin to Chinese Whispers, only with a drawing element. The first person thinks up a sentence (bizarre or surreal works best, with Santa Claus a surprisingly common character) and writes it at the top of a sheet of paper. It is passed to the next person, who must get over the meaning of the sentence with a drawing. The sheet is then folded so that the initial sentence can't be seen and the next player around the table or circle has to write down what they think the picture is trying to communicate.

Naturally, if the original sentence was, "The gorilla passed his driving test with flying colours", the chances are that won't be what the third player writes down.

Santa Hated Mince Pies but still they left them out!

Gregor Samsa woke on Christmas Day to find himself transformed into a giant insect

The Bee Went on Holiday at Christmas

Teddy the snowman should have remembered to tie up the laces on his new rugby ball

It's likely to be even further from the original sentence as the game progresses.

To keep things moving, you can play with several pieces of paper going around at once. Each game you play should end on a sentence. If you want to keep things going for a while longer, you can always stick two sheets of paper together end to end before you begin.

Changing places

Musical Chairs has been a staple of children's parties for decades – here's an updated version that will have both kids and adults joining in the fun.

You need one fewer seats than there are people. Whoever's left standing poses an instruction such as this: "Everyone wearing black socks change places." Everyone to whom this applies must get up and move to a vacant seat. Of course, there will be one person left with nowhere to sit: and that's the person who leads the next round.

Typical phrases might include "Everyone who's been to a supermarket in the last week", "Everyone wearing boxer shorts", "Everyone who hasn't seen the latest Harry Potter film", and so on. Good-natured mayhem results almost immediately, and getting everyone moving around is a great way to break up the typical post-prandial torpor.

I'd be there first if I could reach the chair

As an added twist, we like to include a forfeit – such as singing a song or telling a joke – for anyone who gets it wrong and changes places when they shouldn't. This is a great variation to play after midnight on New Year's Eve, when orders such as "Everyone who's been abroad on holiday this year" will have most people changing places – all in error, of course, since no one will have been anywhere *this* year yet.

The acronym game

This one involves a bit of thought, but it's a good game that involves no moving about or physical exertion of any kind.

Think of a short, well-known word – and then challenge your guests to come up with an acronym (that is, a phrase where the words begin with the letters of the word) that describes the word. So ARM might be Automatic Reaching Mechanism; RING could be Rightful Indicator of Nuptial Gain; SUIT could be Standard Uniform of Interesting Texture, and so on.

Award prizes, if you like, for the best acronym; but it's best played as a collaborative effort, with everyone joining in to find the best solution. Once you've arrived at a phrase that does the job well, move on to the next.

Balance the books

Practical jokes are mean and childish – and this is one of the best.

Explain that you're going to perform a magic trick involving a broom and a stack of books. Climbing up on a chair or table so you can reach the ceiling, you hold the broom in one hand and the stack of books in the other.

Say you need some assistance, and call for help from a volunteer. Give them the broom to hold, the brush end upwards, and position it so the broom is holding the books flat against the ceiling.

Then all you have to do is walk away, leaving the hapless guest unable to move without dropping the books.

If you're feeling particularly brave, reckless or malicious, substitute a plastic bowl full of water for the books. Your victim won't be able to move without getting drenched – to general hilarity!

Peter's presents

This pattern-solving game can be played without rushing about. One player begins by saying: "I'm buying presents for Peter, and I'm giving him a kettle." Each player takes it in turn to think of presents that they might give to Peter – the condition being that the present must follow the rule dreamt up by the first speaker.

It might be that only words with double letters, such as the two Ts in 'kettle' are allowed. In this case, you could also have a bottle, a woollen jumper, a book, a pizza, and so on. You could make a rule that each item has to start with the same letter; or start with the letter with which the previous present ended; or all be the same colour; or contain an unusual letter, such as K.

Once someone has guessed the rule, it's their turn to think up a new one for everyone else to solve. It's important to be consistent: no changing the rules halfway through!

The king and queen of silence

This raucous game originated in France, and is most suitable for larger rooms. It involves a fair amount of preparation, but it's a good active game that gets your guests moving around.

Two players are the king and queen, and they sit at one end of the room. Tradition has it that they wear saucepans on their heads as crowns, although any form of suitable headdress will suffice.

Halfway down the room, build a barricade of chairs, small tables, trays and other furniture. Balanced on these are all the noisy, unbreakable items you can find: saucepans, colanders, brooms, umbrellas, bunches of keys, and so on. Add clothing and cushions to make the game even harder.

At the other end of the room, position the other guests – they're the rabble. One at a time, they must try to cross the barricade, moving items out of the way as necessary, without making any noise. Even the slightest tinkle of keys or clatter of saucepans should be condemned by the king and queen, sending the plebeian miscreants back to the beginning as another peasant has a turn.

It's a remarkably silly game, and one that benefits from local rules that the king and queen can make up as they go along.

Guess who's going to have to clear this mess up

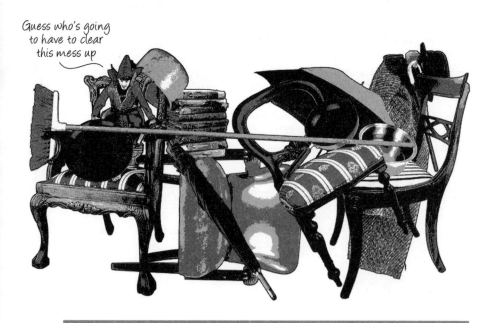

Paper dancing

Players pair up into couples, and dance around a sheet of newspaper. When the music stops, they have to both jump onto the sheet of paper.

So far, it's easy. But then, when the music starts again, the paper is folded in half – and continues to be folded each time. Eventually, you end up with each couple trying desperately to hold each other up as they perch on a tiny sheet of paper that will barely hold their feet. A raucous game for friends who know each other very well – or would like to.

I see the FTSE's fallen again

Masterword

You surely remember the old *Mastermind* board game, where you have to guess the colours of a row of four pegs. This entertaining variation does away with the board and the pegs. With no pieces to lose, the game can be played anywhere.

One player thinks of a three-letter word – let's say, 'hot'. The others then have to guess the word; they're told after each guess how many letters are correct. So if they guess 'dog' they'd be told they have one letter right; if they guess 'top' then two letters are right, and so on. No messing about with letters in the right or wrong position here: if they're in the word, they're correct.

Once you get proficient at this game, try four-letter words instead. It's harder to do, especially for children, but it's a good way for them to learn vocabulary.

First lines

A game to exercise the intellect. One player picks a book from a shelf, and describes its plot to the others. Everyone then has to write on a slip of paper what they believe to be a suitable first sentence; the person who picked the book writes down the real first sentence.

All the sentences are read out, and everyone has to nominate which they think is the authentic one. Score one point if you pick the real first sentence – and an additional point for each player whose made-up sentence is chosen by someone else as the real McCoy.

Winning board games

If you're like us, you only play board games to be sociable and would never dream of trying to win. But if the rest of your family is incredibly competitive, perhaps you wouldn't mind occasionally being the one doing the lap of honour of the living room, tablecloth draped around your shoulders, a candlestick held aloft as a trophy. A little bit of preparation might not hurt, therefore. It's not so much training, as giving them a good game.

Trivial Pursuit

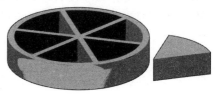

There isn't much by way of strategy in *Trivial Pursuit*. If you have a classics degree and read three newspapers every day, the chances are you'll still lose to somebody who does a pub quiz once in a blue moon. But here are a few handy tips.

- If you visit the hub before you have filled all the segments on your 'cheese', you can choose your category question to keep going.

- If you're trying to land on the hub to complete the game but overshoot it, make sure to land on a square containing a category you like.

- If a rival player needs to answer a hub question to win, choose the category they've had most problems with.

If you think people's attention will flag quickly, don't use the board but simply use the cards to ask questions.

I need to convert this thing to run on unleaded

Monopoly

A game of chance? Not a bit of it. Seasoned *Monopoly* players will beat you hollow every time if you don't know basic strategy. Here are a few tips to help you get your own back.

- The only way you'll win is through collecting rents, so you *must* get a set of streets and build properties as soon as possible. If another player has the one you need for a set, be prepared to pay through the nose for it. As long as nobody else has built on their properties, it won't matter if you spend almost everything you have.

- Build on the property in each set with the highest rent first.

- Whichever country's version of *Monopoly* you play, go first for the orange and red sets. They get the most visits. Light blue and green are the least valuable, though grabbing one of each can be useful for trading later.

- The most efficient return comes from having three houses on each property. One set with two houses is much better than two sets with one.

- The utilities don't offer a good return, and aren't worth the initial expenditure. But stations can be a steady source of income.

- Get out of jail quickly early on. Later in the game, stay there, as you don't have to pay rents.

Cluedo

"Colonel Mustard with the lead piping in the billiard room." Ah, the joy of uttering those accusations in *Cluedo*, invented by Anthony Prat back in 1948.

- Make a note of every suggestion and keep trying to work out what they mean.

- If you move to a room for which you already have the card, it helps to winnow down the possibilities for the murderer and the weapon.

- Don't concentrate on just one of the three elements, though – try to solve all three.

- Slow down other players by continually showing them the same card if you can.

- Mean though it is, if you know where other players want to go, call them into rooms where they don't need to be. It will slow them down, and could give you the edge you need to win.

Scrabble

Strategy and an intimate knowledge of the backwaters of the English language are vital. If you're prepared to put in a little effort, memorise some two-letter words. If you're challenged, point out that they're acceptable even if you can't remember what they mean. So yah boo sucks to them! If you don't want to admit your ignorance, claim it's an old Gaelic, Hindu or Egyptian word. It usually is.

Two-letter words you didn't realise you already knew

Ad	At	Da	Em [1]	Go	Id	La [3]	Mu	[2] Oi	Or	Re [3]	Um	Ye
Ah	Ax	Do	En [1]	Ha	If	Lo	My	Om	Ow	So	Up	Yo
Am	Be	Ef [1]	Er	He	In	Ma	No	On	Ox	Ta	Us	
An	Bi	Eh	Es [1]	Hi	Is	Me	Nu [2]	Oo	Pa	Ti [3]	We	
As	By	El [1]	Fa [3]	Ho	It	Mi [3]	Oh	Op	Pi [2]	To	Xi [2]	

[1] *The letters F, L, M, N and S when spelled out;* [2] *Greek letters;* [3] *As in Doh, Re, Mi!*

Two-letter words you probably didn't know

Aa *lava*

Ae *Scots for 'one'*

Ay *'always' or 'yes'*

Ba *Egyptian religion*

Bo *same as 'boo'*

Ch *old version of 'I'*

Di *plural of 'deus'*

Ea *dialect for 'river'*

Ee *Scots for 'eye'*

Fy *same as 'fie'*

Gi *judo costume*

Gu *Shetland viol*

Io *expression of joy*

Jo *Scots loved one*

Mo *old form of 'more'*

Na *Scots for 'no'*

Ne *old word for 'no'*

Ny *old spelling of 'nigh'*

Ob *an objection*

Od *old word for god*

Oe *same as 'oy'*

Os *a bone*

Ou *Scots concession*

Oy *Scots grandchild*

Ph *degree of acidity*

Po *short chamberpot*

Qi *life force*

Sh *call for silence*

Si *earlier form of 'Ti'*

St *call for silence*

Te *same as 'Ti'*

Ug *to loathe*

Un *dialect for 'one'*

Ur *same as 'Er'*

Ut *same as 'Doh'*

Wo *variant of 'woe'*

Xu *Vietnamese coin*

Yu *precious jade*

Zo *Himalayan cattle*

General Scrabble tips

● Turn the board to face you on your turn or you're unnecessarily making it difficult for yourself.

● Although it's great to put down all seven letters (a 50 point bonus), it's more important to keep scoring than trying to use all your letters. If you're not scoring more than 10 points on most turns, change some letters and miss a go.

 Shuffle the letters on your rack, keeping popular suffixes or prefixes to one side. Aim for a rough balance of vowels and consonants and get rid of duplicates. The best letters to have are those comprising the word RETAINS. They're the most useful for making seven-letter words.

 Use premium point squares whenever possible, trying to place the highest scoring letter in your rack on them. Keep looking for 'hooks', adding letters to words to make new ones – such as '-ing' or plurals.

 J, Q, X and Z are the highest-scoring letters. Play them early, though, or you cut your flexibility. There are 22 ways of playing Q without using U: Qat (a tea-like drug) and Qadi (a Muslim magistrate) are two of the most useful. Don't get stuck with these letters (particularly Z or Q) at the end.

 At the end of the game, play out first to leave your opponent with tiles: you get extra points for all the tiles they still hold.

Scrabble variations

There are some interesting variants on *Scrabble* that lend themselves to a mixed ability family gathering.

 Allow players (or just the children) to consult a dictionary at any point.

 Score additional points for words connected with themes. Add five points, for instance, for every word connected with Christmas.

 In *Scrabble Bingo*, each player picks two seven-letter words that can be made with the letters in the bag (check the instructions to see how many of each letter there are). A neutral person picks letters at random and calls them out, the players crossing out one letter at a time (even if they have the letter more than once). The first person to cross out all their letters calls out "Bingo" and wins the game.

The real cost of Christmas

The song *The Twelve Days of Christmas* is a lengthy shopping list that's guaranteed to turn any true love's head. But what would the cost be if we were daft enough actually to try to buy all those items? Are they even all readily available? Time to go surfing!

A partridge in a pear tree: As wild birds, it's hard to buy live partridges. Your best bet is to go on a game shoot and bag your own, although you'll need to be a crack shot to ensure you just wing them. Most shoots charge by the day, but we found a very reasonable £29 a bird deal from *www.iancoleysporting.co.uk*. Pear trees are readily available: you can get them from just £16.99 from *http://fruit.thompson-morgan.com*.   £45.99

Two turtle doves: Fortunately, doves are always sold in sets of two. £18 a pair from *www.cornwallbirds.co.uk*.   £18.00

Three French hens: Unless you're able to get a special import licence, it's illegal to bring live poultry into this country. However, you can buy ready-plucked birds for €9,95 (around £6.90) from *www.natoora.fr*.   £20.70

Four calling birds: 'Calling birds' are, in fact, thrushes and blackbirds, which are tricky to buy. You can achieve the same effect with much less mess with an Acme Bird Caller – just £10.97 from *www.euro-tackle.net*.   £43.88

Five gold rings: The cost of a gold ring varies enormously. But since we're talking quantity rather than quality, you don't need to overspend. £19.99 will get you a nine carat half eternity ring from *www.argos.co.uk*.   £99.95

Six geese a-laying: You could hang around farmers' auctions in the hope of picking up a few tasty birds. Or get bona fide organic geese from £29 each from *www.peachcroft.co.uk* – and if you ask them nicely, they might just throw in half a dozen free-range goose eggs as well.   £174.00

Seven swans a-swimming: All swans in the UK are owned by the Crown, and are not for sale. Why not do the green thing and sponsor a swan for £12 a year at *www.swanuk.co.uk*.   £84.00

Eight maids a-milking: Milkmaids are hard to come by these days. There just isn't the demand. But how about a print of Vermeer's *The Milkmaid*? A snip at just £16.99 each from *www.artland.co.uk*.   £135.92

Nine ladies dancing: Dance troupes cost the earth. Far cheaper to hire nine strippagrams for the evening. Who knows, you might even be able to persuade them to leave their clothes on. Starting at £50 each from *www.partygrams.co.uk.*   £450.00

Ten lords a-leaping: Bit of a problem, this one. The only known leaping lords are Sebastian Coe and Jeffrey Archer, who both used to be Olympic runners. But they would be a little pricey for an evening's hire, even if they could rustle up eight athletic ermine-clad chums. We suggest you settle for a training session at Lord's Cricket Ground: it's a very reasonable £13.25 per person. Bring your own leapers. Details from *www.lords.org.*   £132.50

Eleven pipers piping: The cost of hiring a bagpiper varies tremendously; you can pay anything from £100 to £350 for a single musician. On the other hand, if you're in the Greater London region £630 will get you a full pipe and drum outfit from *www.piperforhire.co.uk.* And if you can persuade the drummers to hang on until the following day, you'll make a further saving here.   £630

Twelve drummers drumming: Session drummers generally charge around £150 per three-hour stint, plus £25 or so for 'porterage' (that's humping their drum kits around). Best place to book them is *www. musofinder.co.uk*, although we reckon you're better off with a dozen drum machines – at least they have an off switch.   £2,100.00

Grand Total: £3,934.94

Christmas jokes

Three men die on Christmas Eve, and are stopped by St Peter as they stand at the Pearly Gates.

"In keeping with the season," says St Peter, "to enter heaven you must each produce something that symbolises Christmas."

The first man rummages through his pockets and pulls out a lighter. He flicks it on and says, "This represents a candle."

St Peter smiles and says, "You may pass through the Pearly Gates."

The second guy produces a bunch of keys and jangles them. "They're bells," he says.

St Peter smiles and says, "You may pass through the Pearly Gates."

The third man is now looking really panicky. Finally, with a triumphant cry, he produces a pair of knickers from his pocket.

"And just how," says a sceptical St Peter, "do *they* symbolise Christmas?"

"They're Carol's," says the man.

Why is Santa so jolly? Because he knows where all the bad girls live.

Shopping in December, a man saw a fantastic train set. "I'll take it," he told the assistant.

"I'm sure your son will love it," said the assistant.

"You're probably right," said the man. "I'd better have two."

What's the difference between snowmen and snow women?

Snowballs.

Mr and Mrs Smith were touring Russia. Their guide, Rudy, argued all the time. As the couple was leaving Moscow, the husband glanced out of the window of the car and said, "Look, it's snowing out."

The guide disagreed, "No, sir, it's raining."

"Surely it's snowing," said Mr Smith.

Fearing a possible diplomatic incident, his wife decided she had to end the dispute immediately, and said: "Rudolph the Red knows rain, dear."

Why is Christmas just like a day at the office ?

You do all the work and the fat guy with the suit gets all the credit.

Darth Vader tells Luke Skywalker, "I know what you will be getting for Christmas, Luke."

"How come?"

"Because I have felt your presents."

Christmas carols: alternative words

My friends call me Elfis

To the tune of In the Bleak Midwinter

In the bleak mid morning
Gift wrap all around
Christmas just got boring
Now Auntie Joan's come round.

Time to get the Scrabble out
While Mum is burning lunch;
The turkey's toast, the brussels sprouts
Are turning into mush.

A tight embrace in your front room
You know you're out of luck;
That awful smell is Joan's perfume:
Eau de Toilet Duck.

When she's kissed you sloppily
It's off the Richter scale;
After lunch, Monopoly –
I think I'll stay in jail.

To the tune of Away in a Manger

Awoke with a stranger, mince pies in the bed
There are hairs on the pillow, some white and some red
There are damp snowy patches all over the floor
And a red Santa suit on the back of the door

Last night in my bedroom as I lay fast asleep
Someone came down the chimney, and it wasn't a sweep
Now there's soot on the carpet in front of the grate
There are elves in the bathroom, and I'm having to wait

There's a reindeer in the kitchen, and it's making me mad, it
Just shows you what happens when you find that you've had it
Away with a stranger who came through the snow
No wonder old Santa always goes Ho ho ho.

To the tune of Ding Dong Merrily on High

Ding, dong, someone at the door   Bo-o-o-o-o-o-o-ring
The front door bell is ringing   We'll give them bread and honey
Ding, dong, what a crashing bore   Bo-o-o-o-o-o-o-ring
It's carol singers singing   I bet they ask for money.

To the tune of O Little Town of Bethlehem

O little town of Milton Keynes, how still your concrete cows.
They fall in love by artificial means, and swear their concrete vows.
Their hides are always pebble dashed
Their legs are reinforced.
No matter how their dreams are smashed
They'll never get divorced.

To the tune of The First Noël

The first Noël was Coward the sage
Who told Worthington's daughter to keep off the stage
Who brought us mad dogs, and mad Englishmen
And a barrage of humour that flowed from his pen.
Noël, Noël, Noël, Noël,
Coward's the man who pleased us so well.

The second Noël was Edmonds the daft
Whose ghastly House Party ne'er once made us laugh.
His flares and wide lapels were his notable props
When he bored the nation on Top of the Pops.
Noël, Noël, Noël, Noël,
Edmonds has brought us to television hell.

The third Noël was Liam's sibling
Who wrote all the songs that Oasis would sing
What's the Story, Morning Glory, and Wonderwall
But he's stuck with his brother in constant brawl.
Noël, Noël, Noël, Noël,
Two song writers and a dee jay as well.

A holiday named after me? You're too, too kind

Festive puzzles

Brain going a little soft? Sharpen it up with this selection of yuletide logical thinking conundrums to test yourself and your family.

Mouldy logic

The one mince pie you didn't eat on Christmas Day has grown an interesting new form of mould – one that doubles in size every day as the organisms in it divide. By New Year's Day, the mince pie is completely covered in mould. On which day was it half covered?

The innkeeper's solution

The innkeeper in Bethlehem was surprised when 13 guests appeared one Christmas Eve, all demanding a room for the night. He only had 12 rooms, and the stable was already full.

   Not wanting to lose the custom, he found an ingenious solution. He first asked the 13th guest to wait for a while with the first guest in room 1. So there were now two people in the first room. He then took the third guest to room 2, the fourth to room 3, and so on – all the way up to the 12th guest, who went into room 11. Then he returned to room one, and took the 13th guest to the empty room 12. How on earth did he manage it?

Rudolph in the woods

How far can a reindeer run into the forest?

Pet likes

I asked for a pet for Christmas – and was really surprised when I received an assortment of snakes, birds, cats and rabbits! Altogether I counted 15 heads, 6 wings, and 38 legs. How many snakes did I get?

Day to day

Christmas Day and New Year's Day are exactly seven days apart, so always fall on the same day of the week. In the year 2000, however, Christmas Day and New Year's Day fell on different days of the week. Why?

The half-empty bottle

You have, unaccountably, a half-empty wine bottle left over from your celebrations (right). Or rather, it's roughly half empty. Without removing the cork, using only a ruler, how can you tell exactly the proportion of wine remaining in it?

Present dilemma

Under my Christmas tree are a number of presents. All except two are for me. All except two are for my brother. And all except two are for my sister. How many presents are there?

Solutions

Mouldy logic: *It was half covered on New Year's Eve, when it was half the size it is now.*

The Innkeeper's solution: *It's a sleight of hand word trick. The guest moved to room 2 should have been the second, since it was the 13th who waited in room 1.*

Rudolph in the woods: *He can run halfway in. After that, he's running out again.*

Pet likes: *There are six wings, which means three birds. Each has a head and two legs. So that leaves 12 heads and 32 legs. Both rabbits and cats have four legs each; 4 x 8 is 32, so there must be eight cats or rabbits. Which means there must be only four snakes.*

Day to day: *Christmas Day 2000 was near the end of the year. New Year's Day 2000 was, of course, the first day of the year.*

The half-empty bottle: *Measure the height of the wine in the bottle. Then turn it upside down and measure the height of the air space above the wine. This will give you the proportion of air to wine in the bottle. Ingenious!*

Present dilemma: *There are three presents – one each.*

Magic tricks

Everyone loves a magic trick. Here are some great tricks that are easy to do, and that will cement your reputation as a great magician.

Feel the force

In this relatively easy but hugely impressive trick, a member of your audience will randomly pick a card, only to be astounded along with the rest of your family when your victim opens a sealed envelope containing the name of their card.

This piece of magic involves a *force*, a card that your victim believes they have picked entirely at random but which, in fact, you have already chosen for them. All you need to do is preset the card at the bottom of the pack. Suppose it's the nine of hearts. Shuffle the pack, making sure you keep that card on the bottom. The easiest way is to use a 'riffle' shuffle, where the pack is split in two and the corners are interlaced; just ensure that your force card hits the table first.

Place the cards face down. Ask your victim to cut the pack anywhere and place those cards beside the others. You need to create a gap of a few seconds before the cards are touched again. With the two piles in front of you, mention that neither you nor they can possibly know which card they've cut to.

Then say casually that you'd better mark the cut, simultaneously picking up the cards *with the force card on the bottom* and placing them on top of the others at right angles. This should be done very naturally, without giving the impression that anything vital is happening. Avoid saying "Okay?" or "Right?" which are giveaways you're doing something sneaky.

Create another brief gap by pointing out that even if the cards hadn't been shuffled, nobody would know where they'd been cut to. All this must be done in a lackadaisical, couldn't-matter-less manner, the most important thing being those two breaks between the manipulation of the cards. It may seem very obvious to you what you're doing but the audience will be fooled.

Nonchalantly pick up the top block and hold it with the bottom card facing your victim, telling them to concentrate on it. Look the opposite way, as you show the card to the rest of the audience. Make it obvious you're not trying to glimpse it.

Now change gear. Put the cards down and give an impression of intense effort. Make them think this is the 'tricky' bit when, in fact, you're home and dry. This is where the real fun starts and you can milk it for all it's worth.

You are now ready to announce which card they chose. It might be that you

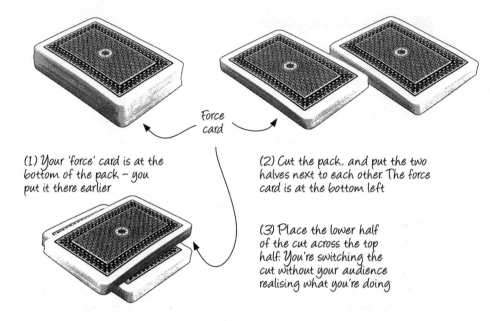

Force
card

(1) *Your 'force' card is at the bottom of the pack – you put it there earlier*

(2) *Cut the pack, and put the two halves next to each other. The force card is at the bottom left*

(3) *Place the lower half of the cut across the top half. You're switching the cut without your audience realising what you're doing*

have a duplicate card sticking out from behind a picture; or maybe you've hidden an envelope on the mantelpiece with a piece of paper saying, "On Boxing Day evening, you will pick a card and it will be the nine of hearts." Or...

- Set up your mobile phone so that, with the press of one button, it sends your victim a text message saying, "The nine of hearts."

- If you've made your own Christmas crackers, keep one aside that is left in open view; get a couple of people to pull it, only to discover that there's a picture of the nine of hearts inside.

- If you want to be really sneaky, get someone in on the trick to take a digital photo of you and your victim earlier, with you holding a hidden nine of hearts; put this somewhere unobtrusive in the room and point to it now.

- If you're hideously rich, have a plane tow a banner behind it, reading, "Nine of hearts." Of course, if you overimbibed and get the trick wrong, this is the point where you're going to look *really* silly.

Martin's magic minion

In this delicious visual trick, invented by our actor chum Martin Ball, your young helper is going to leave the room; they will return by leaping a clear 10ft gap to appear, amazingly, from behind your magic blanket.

The perfect situation is to have a doorway outside which you can 'place' your assistant while, in the room, there's something solid such as a sofa with space behind it. You can use a large cardboard box that contained a big present, though you may need to put a plate of something on it to make it look less out of place.

Making it perfectly clear you're up to something, you and your assistant should be seen going in and out of the room a few times. At the crucial moment, when nobody's paying any attention, your minion ducks into their hiding place.

You now proceed as if your helper is outside the room. Introduce the trick. Stop at one point, go out and whisper an answer to an imagined question, then return.

Magic blanket

Assistant concealed behind sofa

Look over to the door a couple of times as you talk. All this will place your assistant outside the room as far as the audience is concerned.

As you announce that you are going to transport your minion magically across the gap, you should notice that a magic wand has been left in the room. Ask them to hang on while you take it out to your assistant, saying they have forgotten it (it doesn't have to be a magic wand but should be something you have *two* of).

Produce a 'magic' something that is big enough to conceal your assistant, such as a blanket. Show the audience that it conceals nothing and move it around while still talking as if your minion is outside the door. At the crucial moment, bring the tablecloth or whatever alongside the edge of the sofa or cardboard box, enabling your assistant to move behind it.

Keep a mental image of your helper outside the room as you move the tablecloth away from the hiding place so there's a clear gap, your minion moving with it. Now, with a flourish, look to the door, recite your magic incantation, whip the covering away and your young assistant will appear – magically – to have jumped the gap, duplicate magic wand in hand. Choosing a helper who can conceal themselves for a while without giggling and giving away their hiding place is essential!

Supermarket mind reading

A simple trick that depends on the silliness of its solution. Begin by selecting a member of your audience. Ask them if they've been to a supermarket this year. Ask if they've bought anything in a tin. Keep asking more and more detailed questions, until you arrive at a single item – say, a can of tomato soup.

Then, with a fanfare, produce a folded piece of paper from your pocket. Employing all your showmanship, ask them: "Was *this* your can of soup?" – and unfold the paper, to reveal a printed barcode.

This trick never fails to crack people up. And to make it easier to do, here's a barcode you can photocopy:

12 things to do with a Brussels sprout

Love them or loathe them – well, OK, loathe them. They turn up every year, like tone deaf carol singers. What on earth are we to do with these unlovely, unloved byproducts of the vegetable industry?

Here are a few suggestions:

Sprout conkers

Played just like regular conkers, but with sprouts. Has the advantage of games lasting a shorter time. Try with cooked sprouts for an extra challenge.

Sprout cricket

A variation on French Cricket, played with a tennis racket held against the legs. Extra points if the sprout smashes *through* the racket and hits the legs.

Sprout garlands

Sprouts are strung on strings and suspended from your Christmas tree.

Emergency corks

Half a bottle of wine left over? Plug it with a sprout in the neck. Be careful with the corkscrew when you pull it out, though.

Sprout soccer

Table football, in which sprouts (preferably uncooked) are flicked with the fingers between two goals.

Sprout printing

Cut a sprout in half, dip the flat side in poster paint and make pictures from it on sheets of paper.

Hunt the sprout

A number of sprouts are hidden around the house. Any that aren't discovered immediately will make themselves known after a few days.

Sprout soup

You'll need: 1 kilo cooked sprouts, 1 tin good tomato soup. Recipe: throw away the sprouts, and eat the soup.

Brussels juggling

Each sprout represents a separate EC directive. Can you keep all the sprouts in the air without dropping any?

Pooh sprouts

Similar to *Pooh Sticks*, as immortalised by A A Milne. Each player ties an identifiable tag onto a sprout, and drops it over the side of a bridge. First sprout to appear on the other side wins.

Sprout wine

We're sure many good recipes exist to create the perfect vintage. But we can't bring ourselves to try this one. Sorry.

Sprout whine

What the kids do when you try to make them eat the blasted things.

7 Christmas carols: words and music

THERE COMES A TIME after every Christmas lunch when the family is sitting around at a loose end – too bored to play *Monopoly*, not bored enough for the Queen's Speech. Yes, it's singalong time, the one moment in the year when we're sufficiently anaesthetised to forget our inhibitions and render our merriment in song.

The trouble is, no one can remember the words to more than the first couple of lines of most carols. So we've gathered together a selection of the more popular yuletide ditties, with the odd interesting fact thrown in for good measure. Many Christmas carols have alternative lyrics: we've chosen the best-known versions. And because some of them drone on for verse after verse, we've cut some of the lengthier songs down to size.

We've included the tunes and chords for all the carols, in case there's a musician in the house. We've chosen keys that make the music easy to play on both the piano and the guitar; if you play a non-standard instrument, such as the Eb flugelhorn, then you're on your own. In some cases, the chords have been simplified to make the songs easier to sight read.

Adeste fideles (O come, all ye faithful)

We've included the English words – but we reckon it sounds an awful lot better in the original Latin, and it's bound to impress the neighbours when you sing it at the top of your voice.

Adeste fideles,	O come, all ye faithful, joyful and triumphant,
laeti triumphantes.	O Come ye, O come ye, to Bethlehem.
Venite, venite in Bethlehem.	Come and behold Him, born the King of angels;
Natum videte,	*O come, let us adore Him,*
regem angelorum.	*O come, let us adore Him,*
Venite adoremus,	*O come, let us adore Him, Christ the Lord.*
Venite adoremus,	
Venite adoremus, dominum.	God of God, Light of Light,
	Lo! he abhors not the Virgin's womb;
Cantet nunc io,	Very God, begotten not created.
chorus angelorum	*O come, let us adore Him…*
Cantet nunc aula caelestium	
Gloria, gloria, in excelsis Deo.	Sing, choirs of angels, sing in exultation;
Venite adoremus…	Sing, all ye citizens of heaven above!
	Glory to God, In the highest.
Ergo qui natus, die hodierna	*O come, let us adore Him…*
Jesu, tibi sit gloria	
Patris aeterni,	Yea, Lord, we greet thee, born this happy morning;
verbum caro factus.	Jesu, to Thee be glory given;
Venite adoremus…	Word of the Father, now in flesh appearing.
	O come, let us adore Him…

All through the night

Sleep my child and peace attend thee,
All through the night
Guardian angels God will send thee,
All through the night
Soft the drowsy hours are creeping
Hill and vale in slumber sleeping,
I my loving vigil keeping
All through the night.

While the moon her watch is keeping
All through the night
While the weary world is sleeping
All through the night
O'er thy spirit gently stealing
Visions of delight revealing
Breathes a pure and holy feeling
All through the night.

Love, to thee my thoughts are turning
All through the night
All for thee my heart is yearning,
All through the night.
Though sad fate our lives may sever
Parting will not last for ever,
There's a hope that leaves me never,
All through the night.

O come, all ye rebels

Although the words to *O Come, All Ye Faithful* seem innocent enough, there's reason to believe (and that's good enough for us) that it was written in code as a rallying cry to Jacobites to prepare themselves for the rebellion of 1745.

The original manuscript, which was in Latin, includes hidden Jacobite images – among them Scottish thistles and the Stuart cypher. The 'faithful' was a reference to the supporters of Bonnie Prince Charlie, the 'king over the water'.

The hymn was written by John Francis Wade, a plainsong scribe at the English Catholic college in Douai, France, who was a fervent supporter of the Stuart cause.

Away in a manger

Away in a manger, no crib for a bed,
the little Lord Jesus laid down his sweet head.
The stars in the bright sky looked down where he lay,
the little Lord Jesus asleep on the hay.

The cattle are lowing, the baby awakes,
but little Lord Jesus no crying he makes.
I love you, Lord Jesus; look down from the sky,
and stay by my side until morning is nigh.

Be near me, Lord Jesus, I ask you to stay
close by me for ever, and love me, I pray.
Bless all the dear children in your tender care,
and take us to heaven, to live with you there.

Luther's liturgy

Legend has it that this little ditty was penned by religious reformer Martin Luther, who knocked it off in between nailing pieces of paper to church doors. Sadly, it isn't true – the misconception arose because the hymn first appeared in a Lutheran Sunday school book, published in 1885. The music was composed by William J Kirkpatrick, in 1895.

The words are, though, rather fanciful. There's no mention of cattle being present in any of the four gospels, and the notion that the infant Jesus abstained from screaming his lungs out is pure invention.

Deck the halls with boughs of holly

Deck the halls with boughs of holly
Fa la la la la, la la la la
'Tis the season to be jolly,
Fa la la la la, la la la la

Fill the mead cup, drain the barrel,
Fa la la la la, la la la la
Troll the ancient Yuletide carol,
Fa la la la la, la la la la

See the flowing bowl before us
Fa la la la la, la la la la
Strike the harp and join the chorus
Fa la la la la, la la la la

Follow me in merry measure
Fa la la la la, la la la la
While I sing of beauty's treasure
Fa la la la la, la la la la

Fast away the old year passes,
Fa la la la la, la la la la
Hail the new, ye lads and lasses,
Fa la la la la, la la la la

Laughing, quaffing, all together,
Fa la la la la, la la la la
Heedless of the wind and weather,
Fa la la la la, la la la la

Ding dong! merrily on high

Ding dong! merrily on high
In heav'n the bells are ringing
Ding, dong! verily the sky
Is riv'n with angels singing

Glo-o-o-o-o-o-oria,
Hosanna in excelsis.

E'en so here below, below
Let steeple bells be swungen
And i-o, i-o, i-o
By priest and people be sungen

Glo-o-o-o-o-o-oria,
Hosanna in excelsis.

Pray ye dutifully prime
Your matin chime, ye ringers
May ye beautifully rime
Your evetime song, ye singers

Glo-o-o-o-o-o-oria,
Hosanna in excelsis.

Er...

Many Christmas carols have had new lyrics written to them, mainly by wayward schoolboys who want to be subversive at carol services. There's a great version of this one, which starts:

Big dong in between my thighs
In heaven my balls are ringing…

But we're far too polite to mention it in this book.

The first Noël

The first Noël the angel did say
Was to certain poor shepherds
    in fields as they lay:
In fields where they lay
    a-keeping their sheep
On a cold winter's night
    that was so deep.
Noël, Noël, Noël, Noël,
Born is the King of Israel.

They looked up and saw a star,
Shining in the east, beyond them far:
And to the earth it gave great light,
And so it continued
    both day and night.
Noël, Noël, Noël, Noël,
Born is the King of Israel.

And by the light of that same star
Three wise men came from
    country far;
To seek for a King was their intent,
and to follow the star wherever it went.
Noël, Noël, Noël, Noël,
Born is the King of Israel.

This star drew nigh to the north-west;
O'er Bethlehem it took its rest,
And there it did both stop and stay,
Right over the place where Jesus lay.
Noël, Noël, Noël, Noël,
Born is the King of Israel.

Then entered in those wise men three,
Fell reverently upon their knee,
And offered there in his presence
Their gold and myrrh and
    frankincense.
Noël, Noël, Noël, Noël,
Born is the King of Israel.

Then let us all with one accord
Sing praises to our heav'nly Lord,
That hath made heaven
    and earth of naught,
And with his blood
    mankind has bought.
Noël, Noël, Noël, Noël,
Born is the King of Israel.

God rest ye merry, gentlemen

God rest ye merry, gentlemen,
Let nothing you dismay
Remember Christ our saviour
Was born on Christmas Day
To save us all from Satan's power
When we were gone astray:

O tidings of comfort and joy
Comfort and joy
O tidings of comfort and joy

From God our heav'nly Father
A blessed angel came
And unto certain shepherds
Brought tidings of the same,
How that in Bethlehem was born
The Son of God by name:

O tidings of comfort and joy...

The shepherds at those tidings
Rejoiced much in mind,
And left their flocks a-feeding,
In tempest, storm, and wind,
And went to Bethlehem straightway
This blessed babe to find:

O tidings of comfort and joy...

But when to Bethlehem they came,
Whereat this infant lay
They found him in a manger,
Where oxen feed on hay;
His mother Mary kneeling,
Unto the Lord did pray:

O tidings of comfort and joy...

Now to the Lord sing praises,
All you within this place,
And with true love and brotherhood
Each other now embrace;
This holy tide of Christmas
All others doth deface:

O tidings of comfort and joy...

Merry? Very!

This isn't a song about drunken revellers, despite the apparent name. 'God rest ye merry' was an old greeting, 'rest' having the sense of 'keep'. So the injunction was for God to keep the gentlemen happy.

Sometimes the punctuation police are right!

Good King Wenceslas

Good King Wenceslas looked out
On the Feast of Stephen
When the snow lay round about
Deep and crisp and even.
Brightly shone the moon that night
Though the frost was cruel
When a poor man came in sight
Gathering winter fuel.

"Hither, page, and stand by me
If though know'st it, telling
Yonder peasant, who is he?
Where and what his dwelling?"
"Sire, he lives a good league hence,
Underneath the mountain;
Right against the forest fence,
By Saint Agnes' fountain."

"Bring me flesh, and bring me wine
Bring me pine logs hither.
Thou and I will see him dine
When we bear them thither."
Page and monarch, forth they went
Forth they went together.
Thro' the rude wind's wild lament
And the bitter weather.

"Sire, the night is darker now,
And the wind blows stronger;
Fails my heart, I know not how,
I can go no longer."
"Mark my footsteps, my good page,
Tread thou in them boldly;
Though shalt find the winter's rage
Freeze thy blood less coldly."

In his master's steps he trod,
Where the snow lay dinted;
Heat was in the very sod
Which the Saint had printed.
Therefore, Christian men, be sure,
Wealth or rank possessing,
Ye who now will bless the poor,
Shall yourself find blessing.

The peasant's dilemma

So here's this peasant, who has braved the cruel frost and rude wind to gather winter fuel. As the page tells the king, he lives 'a good league hence'. But then he goes on to inform us that the peasant lives 'right against the forest fence'.

So what's he doing wandering about in the snow? Why can't he just pick up sticks from the forest next door? And, rather than taking flesh and wine to the peasant, wouldn't it have been a kinder gesture for Wenceslas to invite the chap in from the cold?

Hark! The Herald Angels sing

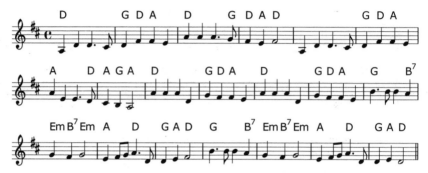

Hark! the Herald Angels sing,
Glory to the new-born King,
Peace on earth and mercy mild,
God and sinner reconcil'd.
Hark! the Herald Angels sing,
Glory to the new-born King.

Beecham's version

The conductor Sir Thomas Beecham was born into the family that manufactured Beecham's Pills, whose laxative powers have kept the country moving since 1842. The company wholeheartedly embraced advertising, and produced – among other things – a book of Christmas carols.

One Christmas, Thomas' father said, "Look here, my lad. I've been spending a lot of brass on your musical education. It's about time we put it to some use. Go through the Annual and tweak some of the verses so as to promote the business." This is one of young Beecham's efforts:

Hark the Herald Angels sing
Beecham's Pills are just the thing,
Two for a woman, one for a child…
Peace on Earth and mercy mild!

In 1936, when Edward VIII abdicated in order to marry Mrs Wallis Simpson, the words were changed again: "Hark the Herald Angels Sing, Mrs Simpson's Pinched our King."

Joyful all ye nations rise,
Join the triumph of the skies,
With the angelic host proclaim,
Christ is born in Bethlehem.
Hark! the Herald Angels sing,
Glory to the new-born King.

Christ by highest Heaven ador'd,
Christ the everlasting Lord!
Late in time behold him come,
Offspring of a Virgin's womb.
Hark! the Herald Angels sing,
Glory to the new-born King.

Hail the Heav'n-born Prince of Peace!
Hail the Sun of righteousness!
Light and life to all he brings,
Risen with healing in his wings.
Hark! the Herald Angels sing,
Glory to the new-born King.

Mild he lays his glory by,
Born that man no more may die,
Born to raise the sons of earth,
Born to give them second birth.
Hark! the Herald Angels sing,
Glory to the new-born King.

The holly and the ivy

The holly and the ivy,
When they are both full grown,
Of all the trees that are in the wood,
The holly bears the crown.

The rising of the sun,
And the running of the deer,
The playing of the merry organ,
Sweet singing in the choir.

The holly bears a blossom
As white as lily flower;
And Mary bore sweet Jesus Christ
To be our sweet Saviour.

Cheerless Charlie

The words to *Hark! the Herald Angels Sing* were written in 1739 by Charles Wesley, whose brother John founded the Methodist church. A thoroughly joyless man, he chose the most miserable tune he could find for his dirge.

A hundred years later, the musician William H Cummings adapted a piece of music by Felix Mendelssohn to give the hymn a more upbeat feel. Mendelssohn had written the tune as a cantata in 1840, to celebrate Gutenberg's invention of the printing press.

The rising of the sun…

The holly bears a berry
As red as any blood;
Any Mary bore sweet Jesus Christ
To do poor sinners good.

The rising of the sun…

The holly bears a prickle
As sharp as any thorn;
And Mary bore sweet Jesus Christ
On Christmas Day in the morn.

The rising of the sun…

The holly bears a bark
As bitter as any gall;
And Mary bore sweet Jesus Christ
For to redeem us all.

The rising of the sun…

The holly and the ivy,
When they are both full grown,
Of all the trees that are in the wood,
The holly bears the crown.

I saw three ships

I saw three ships come sailing in
On Christmas Day, on Christmas Day
I saw three ships come sailing in
On Christmas Day in the morning.

And what was in those ships all three
On Christmas Day, on Christmas Day?
And what was in those ships all three
On Christmas Day in the morning?

Mary mild and Christ were there
On Christmas Day, on Christmas Day
Mary mild and Christ were there
On Christmas Day in the morning.

And all the bells on earth did ring
On Christmas Day, on Christmas Day
And all the bells on earth did ring
On Christmas Day in the morning.

And all the angels in heav'n did sing
On Christmas Day, on Christmas Day
And all the angels in heav'n did sing
On Christmas Day in the morning.

Then let us all rejoice again
On Christmas Day, on Christmas Day
Then let us all rejoice again
On Christmas Day in the morning!

In the bleak mid-winter

In the bleak mid-winter
Frosty wind made moan,
Earth stood hard as iron,
Water like a stone;
Snow had fallen, snow on snow,
Snow on snow,
In the bleak mid-winter
Long ago.

Our God, heav'n cannot hold him
Nor earth sustain;
Heaven and earth shall flee away
When he comes to reign:
In the bleak mid-winter
A stable-place sufficed
The Lord God Almighty,
Jesus Christ.

Enough for him, whom cherubim
Worship night and day,
A breastful of milk
And a mangerful of hay;
Enough for him, whom angels
Fall down before,
The ox and ass and camel
Which adore.

Angels and archangels
May have gathered there,
Cherubim and seraphim
Thronged the air,
But only his mother
In her maiden bliss,
Worshipped the beloved
With a kiss.

What can I give him,
Poor as I am?
If I were a shepherd
I would bring a lamb,
If I were a wise man
I would do my part,
Yet what I can I give him,
Give my heart.

Not all that bleak

So Jesus was born in a snowstorm, eh? Where did they get that idea? The words to this puzzling carol are by the poet Christina Rossetti, who clearly let her artistic licence get the better of her.

The tune is by the noted composer Gustav Holst, who wrote it for *The English Hymnal* in 1906. He called it *Cranham*, after the village near Cheltenham in which he was born.

Jingle bells

Dashing through the snow
In a one-horse open sleigh
Through the fields we go
Laughing all the way.
Bells on bob-tail ring
Making spirits bright
What fun it is to ride and sing
A sleighing song tonight.

Jingle bells, jingle bells
Jingle all the way,
Oh what fun it is to ride
In a one-horse open sleigh, Oh –
Jingle bells…

A day or two ago
I thought I'd take a ride
And soon Miss Fanny Bright
Was seated by my side;
The horse was lean and lank
Misfortune seemed his lot,
We ran into a drifted bank
And there we got upsot.

Jingle bells…

A day or two ago
The story I must tell
I went out on the snow
And on my back I fell;
A gent was riding by
In a one-horse open sleigh
He laughed at me as I there lay
But quickly drove away.

Jingle bells…

Now the ground is white,
Go it while you're young,
Take the girls along
And sing this sleighing song.
Just bet a bob-tailed bay,
Two-forty as his speed,
Hitch him to an open sleigh
And crack! You'll take the lead.

Jingle bells…

Joy to the world

Joy to the world, the Lord is come!
Let earth receive her King;
Let every heart prepare Him room,
Let every heart prepare Him room,
And Heaven and nature sing,
And Heaven and nature sing,
And Heaven, and Heaven,
  and nature sing.

Joy to the earth, the Saviour reigns!
Let men their songs employ;
While fields and floods, rocks, hills
  and plains
While fields and floods, rocks, hills
  and plains
Repeat the sounding joy,
Repeat the sounding joy,
Repeat, repeat, the sounding joy.

No more let sins and sorrows grow,
Nor thorns infest the ground;
He comes to make His blessings flow
He comes to make His blessings flow
Far as the curse is found,
Far as the curse is found,
Far as, far as, the curse is found.

He rules the world with truth and
  grace,
And makes the nations prove
The glories of His righteousness,
The glories of His righteousness,
And wonders of His love,
And wonders of His love,
And wonders, wonders, of His love.

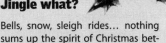

Jingle what?

Bells, snow, sleigh rides... nothing sums up the spirit of Christmas better than *Jingle Bells*.

Except that it wasn't written for Christmas at all. The Boston minister James Pierpoint wrote it in 1857 for children attending his Sunday School Thanksgiving. But it was so popular it was repeated at Christmas, and has stuck there ever since.

O come Emmanuel

O come, O come, Emmanuel
And ransom captive Israel
That mourns in lonely exile here
Until the Son of God appears

Rejoice! Rejoice! Emmanuel
Shall come to thee O Israel

O come, thou rod of Jesse, free
Thine own from Satan's tyranny
From depths of hell thy people save
And give them vict'ry o'er the grave

Give generously,
I'm saving for a
pair of legs

Rejoice! Rejoice! Emmanuel
Shall come to thee O Israel

O come, O dayspring, come and cheer
Our spirits by thine advent here
And drive away the shaves of night
And pierce the clouds and bring us
    light

Rejoice! Rejoice! Emmanuel
Shall come to thee O Israel

O come, thou key of David, come
And open wide our heavenly home
Make safe the way that leads on high
And close the path to misery
Rejoice! Rejoice! Emmanuel
Shall come to thee O Israel

O come, O come, thou Lord of might
Who to thy tribes, on Sinai's height
In ancient times did'st give the law
In cloud and majesty and awe

Rejoice! Rejoice! Emmanuel
Shall come to thee O Israel

O little town of Bethlehem

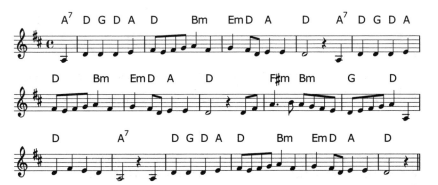

O little town of Bethlehem
How still we see thee lie
Above thy deep and dreamless sleep
The silent stars go by
Yet in the dark streets shineth
The everlasting light
The hopes and fears
Of all the years
Are met in thee tonight.

For Christ is born of Mary,
And gathered all above
While mortals sleep the angels keep
Their watch of wondering love
O morning stars together
Proclaim the holy birth
And praises sing to God the king
And peace to men on earth.

How silently, how silently,
The wondrous gift is given
So God imparts to human hearts
The blessings of his heaven
No ear may hear his coming,
But in this world of sin
Where meek souls will
Receive him still,
The dear Christ enters in.

O holy Child of Bethlehem
Descend to us we pray
Cast out our sin and enter in
Be born in us today
We hear the Christmas angels
The great glad tidings tell
O come to us, abide with us
Our lord Emmanuel.

O little tune that nobody wrote

The words to this song are by Phillips Brooks, the Bishop of Massachusetts, who was inspired to write it on a visit to the Holy Land. The tune is really known as *Forest Green*, and was composed by Vaughan Williams. Except he didn't really write it: he heard a farm labourer in the village of Forest Green, Surrey, singing the traditional ballad *The Ploughman's Dream*, and simply wrote it down.

Once in royal David's city

Once in royal David's city
Stood a lowly cattle shed,
Where a mother laid her baby
In a manger for his bed.
Mary was that mother mild,
Jesus Christ her little child.

He came down to earth from heaven,
Who is God and Lord of all,
And his shelter was a stable,
And his cradle was a stall.
With the poor and mean and lowly
Lived on earth our saviour holy.

And our eyes at last shall see him
Through his own redeeming love,
For that child so dear and gentle
Is our Lord in heaven above.
And he leads his children on
To the place where he is gone.

I wasn't sure about
the myrrh, so I've kept
the receipt

Silent night

Silent night! Holy night! | Stille Nacht! Heilige Nacht!
All is calm, all is bright | Alles schläft; einsam wacht
Round yon virgin mother and child, | Nur das traute hoch heilige Paar.
Holy infant so tender and mild, | Holder Knab' im lockigen Haar,
Sleep in heavenly peace! | Schlafe in himmlischer Ruh'!
Sleep in heavenly peace! | Schlafe in himmlischer Ruh'!

Silent night! Holy night!
Shepherds quake at the sight;
Glories stream from heaven afar,
Heavenly hosts sing alleluia,
Christ, the saviour, is born!
Christ, the saviour, is born!

Stille Nacht! Heilige Nacht!
Gottes Sohn, o wie lacht
Lieb' aus deinem göttlichen Mund,
Da schlägt uns die rettende Stund'.
Jesus in deiner Geburt!
Jesus in deiner Geburt!

Silent night! Holy night!
Son of God, love's pure light
Radiant beams from thy holy face,
With the dawn of redeeming grace,
Jesus, Lord at thy birth,
Jesus, Lord at thy birth.

Stille Nacht! Heilige Nacht!
Die der Welt Heil gebracht,
Aus des Himmels goldenen Höhn
Uns der Gnaden Fülle läßt seh'n:
Jesus in Menschengestalt,
Jesus in Menschengestalt.

Mohr or less true

In the winter of 1818, the priest Joseph Mohr was about to celebrate Christmas in the tiny Austrian village of Oberndorf, when he discovered that a mouse had nibbled through the organ wiring. Aghast at the thought of there being no music, Mohr dug up an old poem of his and arranged it so it could be played on a guitar. Like many such legends, this one's not true. But we've included the German words anyway, because they sound so much better.

The twelve days of Christmas

On the first day of Christmas,
My true love gave to me:
A partridge in a pear tree.

On the second day of Christmas,
My true love gave to me:
Two turtle doves,
And a partridge in a pear tree.

On the third day of Christmas,
My true love gave to me:
Three french hens,

Two turtle doves,
And a partridge in a pear tree.

On the fourth day of Christmas,
My true love gave to me:
Four calling birds,
Three french hens,
Two turtle doves,
And a partridge in a pear tree.

On the fifth day of Christmas,
My true love gave to me:

Five gold rings!
Four calling birds,
Three french hens,
Two turtle doves,
And a partridge in a pear tree.

On the sixth day of Christmas,
My true love gave to me:
Six geese a-laying,
Five gold rings...

On the seventh day of Christmas,
My true love gave to me:
Seven swans a-swimming,
Six geese a-laying,
Five gold rings...

On the eighth day of Christmas,
My true love gave to me:
Eight maids a-milking,
Seven swans a-swimming,
Six geese a-laying,
Five gold rings...

On the ninth day of Christmas,
My true love gave to me:
Nine ladies dancing,
Eight maids a-milking,
Seven swans a-swimming,
Six geese a-laying,
Five gold rings...

On the tenth day of Christmas,
My true love gave to me:
Ten lords a-leaping,
Nine ladies dancing,
Eight maids a-milking,
Seven swans a-swimming,
Six geese a-laying,
Five gold rings...

On the eleventh day of Christmas,
My true love gave to me:
Eleven pipers piping,
Ten lords a-leaping,
Nine ladies dancing,
Eight maids a-milking,
Seven swans a-swimming,
Six geese a-laying,
Five gold rings...

On the twelfth day of Christmas,
My true love gave to me:
Twelve drummers drumming,
Eleven pipers piping,
Ten lords a-leaping,
Nine ladies dancing,
Eight maids a-milking,
Seven swans a-swimming,
Six geese a-laying,
Five gold rings!
Four calling birds,
Three french hens,
Two turtle doves,
And a partridge in a pear tree.

What does it mean?

Some say these words are all religious imagery: the partridge is Jesus on the cross, the two turtle doves are the Old and New Testaments, and so on. It gets a little silly: the nine ladies dancing are claimed to be the nine fruits of the Holy Spirit (Galatians 5:22, if you want to look them up).

In fact, this is all probably nonsense. They're just good lyrics.

While shepherds watched their flocks by night

While shepherds watch their flocks by
    night
All seated on the ground
The angel of the Lord came down
And glory shone around

"Fear not," said he (for mighty dread
had seized their troubled mind)
"Glad tidings of great joy I bring
To you and all mankind.

"To you in David's town this day
Is born of David's line
A saviour who is Christ the Lord
And this shall be the sign

"The heav'nly babe you there shall find
To human view displayed
All meanly wrapped in swathing bands
And in a manger laid."

Thus spoke the seraph and forthwith
Appeared a shing throng
Of angels praising God who thus
Addressed their joyful song:

"All glory be to God on high
And on the earth be peace
Goodwill henceforth from heav'n to
    men
Begin and never cease."

The debtor's hymn

The story of the Annunciation to the shepherds comes from the gospel of St Luke. This hymn was written by the poet Nahum Tate, whose main claim to fame was the rewriting of Shakespeare's *King Lear* to give it a happy ending.

Tate's best known poem was *Panacea*, an ode to tea. He should have taken his own advice: Tate became an alcoholic, and died in a debtor's prison in 1715.

The only Christmas hymn to be approved for inclusion in a collection of psalms produced under royal warrant in 1700, *While Shepherds* has been sung to over 100 different tunes. This, the most popular, is known as *Winchester Old*, which first appeared in a psalm book published in 1592.

We three kings

We three kings of Orient are,
Bearing gifts we traverse afar,
Field and fountain, moor and
   mountain,
Following yonder star.

O, star of wonder, star of might,
Star with royal beauty bright,
Westward leading, still proceeding,
Guide us to thy perfect light.

Born a babe on Bethlehem's plain;
Gold we bring to crown Him again;
King forever, ceasing never,
Over us all to reign.

O, star of wonder…

Frankincense to offer have I;
Incense owns a Deity nigh;
Prayer and praising, all men raising,
Worship Him, God on High.

O, star of wonder…

Myrrh is mine; its bitter perfume
Breathes a life of gathering gloom;
Sorrowing, sighing, bleeding, dying,
Seal'd in the stone-cold tomb.

O, star of wonder…

Glorious now behold Him arise,
King and God and sacrifice,
Heaven sings, "Hallelujah!"
"Hallejujah!" Earth replies.

O, star of wonder…

We three…

Few carols have more alternative versions than this one. Our favourites are:

We four Beatles of Liverpool are,
John in a taxi, Paul in a car,
George on a scooter, beeping his hooter
Following Ringo Starr.

And the ever-popular:

We three kings of Leicester Square
Selling ladies' underwear
It's fantasic
No elastic
Only a penny a pair!

We wish you a Merry Christmas

We wish you a Merry Christmas
We wish you a Merry Christmas
We wish you a Merry Christmas
And a Happy New Year.

Good tidings we bring
To you and your kin
We wish you a Merry Christmas
And a Happy New Year.

Oh, bring us a figgy pudding
Oh, bring us a figgy pudding
Oh, bring us a figgy pudding
And a cup of good cheer.

Good tidings we bring
To you and your kin
We wish you a Merry Christmas
And a Happy New Year.

We won't go until we've got some
We won't go until we've got some
We won't go until we've got some
So bring some out here.

Good tidings we bring
To you and your kin
We wish you a Merry Christmas
And a Happy New Year.

We wish you a Merry Christmas
We wish you a Merry Christmas
We wish you a Merry Christmas
And a Happy New Year.

Sorry about that, it's the figgy pudding

8 Happy New Year

CHRISTMAS HAS COME AND GONE: the turkey's shredded, the wrapping paper binned, most of the toys are broken and those that are left have run out of batteries, despite your best efforts to stock up this year.

But before the long, hard slog of winter sets in, there's one festive occasion remaining: New Year's Eve. Frequently less fraught and more relaxed than Christmas itself, it's a time when the jollity doesn't need to be forced, and when goodwill spreads itself around like a fine dusting of snow.

But even New Year's Eve is rife with difficulty. How do you assemble that bow tie that hasn't seen the light of day since this time last year? How do you keep your guests entertained when things begin to flag? And at what point should you link crossed arms when singing *Auld Lang Syne*?

All good things must come to an end, and the Christmas period is no exception. Start your new year on a good footing, with tips on what to do with those unwanted gifts and old Christmas cards, and some useful ideas on how to turn the sales to your advantage.

How to tie a bow tie

As any aficionado of the form will tell you, tying a bow tie is easy. Well, it isn't. It takes practice, and even experts may have to tie it several times before it looks right. However, there's nothing to beat the rakish, devil-may-care appearance you get from *untying* it halfway through the evening and letting the loose ends drape over your shirt. Try doing *that* with a clip-on!

We recognise that not all of us can call on our valet for assistance in this matter. So here's a quick guide for those whose gentlemen's gentlemen have been given New Year's Eve off.

1 First make a standard knot, as if you were beginning a shoelace, with one end of the tie hanging down (**A**) and the other (**B**) held up in the air. The tail on end **B**, where it joins the rest of the tie, should be an inch or so longer than end **A**.

2 Loop end **B** back on itself and up in the air. Simon drapes this end on his shoulder; Steve holds it in his teeth. Jeeves doubtless wouldn't approve – but remember you foolishly gave him permission to go off and frolic in the Trafalgar Square fountains.

3 Fold end **A** at the point where the thick end joins the main part of the bow tie, so that it doubles back on itself, and push this folded end through the loop formed by the tail of end **B**.

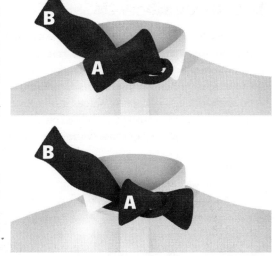

4 This will form the front of the tie. Push it halfway through the loop, then pull end **B** to hold it all in place.

5 Fold **B** back on itself – in other words, towards you – and push through the loop in front of the original knot at the back of the tie.

6 All that remains is for you to pull, tweak and twist on the ends of the tie until the whole assembly resembles one of those clip-on johnnies you wish you'd bought in the first place. Don't be disheartened if it doesn't work first time – it can take a little practice to get it exactly right. But think of the admiration that will be yours when you undo the damn thing later on!

Is it safe to come out now?

Twelfth Night

The Twelve Days of Christmas actually begin on Christmas Night (the first night), so that Twelfth Night is the evening of January 5th and the day of January 6th. In Tudor times, it marked the end of the winter festival overseen by the King or Lord of Misrule, which ran from All Hallows Eve (Halloween). The idea of turning things on their head, with masters waiting on servants and people dressing up as the opposite sex, was explored in Shakespeare's *Twelfth Night* and continues to this day: the principal boy in panto is often played by a woman, while the Dame is always a man.

Twelfth Night used to be a time of boisterous celebrations, originally intended to frighten away evil spirits. What we think of as Christmas cake was originally served then. Traditionally, this Twelfth Cake contained a bean, and whoever got it was crowned King or Queen of the Bean and – irrespective of their normal station in life – could order everybody to do silly things.

Now the only way we mark Twelfth Night is by taking down the Christmas decorations. Failure to do so on that day will bring bad luck, it's said, and the only way to avoid it is to leave them up all year. Bang goes the New Year's resolution for keeping the place tidy, then.

Christmas card basketball

Taking Christmas cards down can be a mite depressing: it heralds the prospect of yet another long, cold winter with little festive joy in sight. But the fun doesn't have to be over quite yet.

My family think I'm a champion tosser

Set two or more players' chairs a couple of yards away from a large waste basket or laundry hamper. Each player should take half a dozen Christmas cards and, in turn, try to throw them into the target.

It's very much harder than it sounds. If only cards were more aerodynamic!

The New Year's Honours List

The honours system has evolved out of the medieval Orders of Chivalry. Twice a year, on the Queen's birthday and at New Year, gongs are given out to the great and/or the good.

The top award, omitting weird things like Most Noble Orders of Garters and Thistles, are the Knights and Dames (who included Tom Jones and Vivienne Westwood in 2006).

The majority of honours belong to the Order of the British Empire, instituted by George V in 1917. Below the Knights are Commanders of the British Empire (CBE: Bruce Forsyth, Peter Snow), Officer of the British Empire (OBE: Gordon Ramsay, Robbie Coltrane) and Member of the British Empire (MBE: Roy Barraclough, The Beverley Sisters).

If you're looking for your own name on New Year's Day, it's too late – you would have been notified well in advance. Unless you really *are* there, of course.

Decorations: the sales advantage

There are some things that should be done before Christmas – and there are some things that should be done *well* before Christmas. A couple of days after the previous Christmas, in fact.

That's when the January sales start. Sure, you can queue up for your cut-price washing machines and gold necklaces, but if you're after real bargains then check out the Christmas decorations trade. Shopkeepers have boxes and boxes of the stuff they're desperate to get rid of: after all, they don't want to have to store it for another whole year.

As well as DIY stores and supermarkets, upmarket chains such as Paperchase put virtually their entire range of decorations on sale for half price, sometimes even offering a 75 per cent discount to shift the last stubborn remnants. You can pick up high-quality, low-cost baubles, glitter cans, lights, tinsel and other trinkets without the hurly burly of high street sales. You'll probably have the store to yourself: after all, who in their right mind would buy decorations at this time of year?

There are only two catches: you have to remember to buy them a year before you need them; and you have to remember a year later where you put the pesky things.

I came, I saw, I partied

The origins of the New Year

New Year was first celebrated by the ancient Babylonians around 2000 BC. The date was set as the first new moon after the vernal equinox: in other words, the first day of spring.

The Romans observed the new year in March, but continued tinkering with the calendar by successive emperors meant that the date no longer tallied with the sun's movements. In 153 BC, the Senate set January 1 as the first day of the year; but still the emperors messed about with the months. In 46 BC, Julius Caesar devised the Julian calendar, which again set January 1 as the beginning of the year. In order to put this date back in line with the sun, however, he had to let the previous year linger on for a total of 445 days.

It was also the Babylonians who invented New Year's resolutions – and the most popular resolution was to return borrowed farm equipment. So when your neighbour asks for his mower back on New Year's Day, he's helping you to enact an ancient ritual.

The gift that keeps giving

One of the busiest times for online auction house eBay is just after the Christmas holiday period. Listings soar for items such as women's sweaters, books, videos and of course fitness equipment, many of them gifts that were "absolutely wonderful" – but not quite so wonderful that the recipients want to hang onto them for a moment longer than necessary.

If the aim of a gift is to give pleasure, then is there anything wrong with this? It might not just be that you don't like the present. You may already have one, but don't want to hurt the donor's feelings by telling them.

Slightly shadier, perhaps, is the practice of 'regifting': passing a present onto somebody else while pretending that you bought it for them. Over half of Americans and around a quarter of Britons own up to regifting, which means the figures are probably far higher. 'Regifting' is, incidentally, a word introduced to the language in a 1995 episode of *Seinfeld*.

If you *are* going to pass on a present as your own, there are a few elementary precautions to take:

● Ensure that there is nothing to show that the item was originally intended for you. If it's an engraved silver tankard, you may be in trouble here.

● Discard the wrapping. Not only might it look tatty but it may conceal something slipped inside that would give the game away. The consequences of giving your mother-in-law a fondue set with a gift tag saying "To Peter with love from Uncle Matthew" are too horrible to contemplate.

● Never admit what you're doing. Telling anyone you're giving them something you didn't want yourself will win you no brownie points and is merely likely to sour the moment, even if a maroon sweater with yellow daisies is exactly what they wanted. If you wore it throughout the holidays before deciding to give it away then a charity shop is the right recipient, not a close member of your family. Even if you *have* managed to sponge the cranberry sauce stains off.

● Most importantly of all, make sure you keep track of who gave you any item you may conceivably regift in the future. This is particularly important if you keep a stack of stuff to use as presents at some indeterminate date. If there is anything worse than leaving the original gift tag on, it must surely be the way the grin is wiped off your face when you hand somebody a present they originally gave you. Similarly, giving it to somebody who knows the original donor could backfire spectacularly.

Card recycling

If you ever find yourself buying gift tags for presents, the chances are they're made out of old Christmas cards. Instead of throwing yours away after Twelfth Night, hang onto them. Either now, or towards next Christmas, get the kids to help cut out the prettiest pictures from the cards. Don't just stick to rectangular shapes. Get them to try their hand at triangles, hearts, stars or circles as well.

Make a hole with a punch in a corner and thread a few inches of ribbon through and you have your own gift tags.

New Year's traditions around the world

Amazingly, there are New Year's traditions other than dancing in fountains and painting the pavement with pizza. Here are some of the more colourful and entertaining global habits.

The best-known tradition in **Scotland**, where Hogmanay is taken very seriously, is that of *first-footing* – trying to be the first person in the year to enter the home of a friend or neighbour. The first-footer should bring gifts: a piece of coal to symbolise warmth was the most common, though these days it's just as likely to be a bottle or a box of chocolates left from the previous few days' celebrations.

The first-footer is supposed to bring luck and those who are tall and dark are thought to bring the best fortune (possibly dating back to the days of Viking raids, when the sudden arrival of a tall blond stranger might not have been so welcome!). In return for the gifts, the first-footer will usually be offered food and drink. First-footing can turn into something akin to a pub crawl, as a group of increasingly merry revellers visits the homes of everyone they know.

In **Stonehaven** in north-east Scotland a procession of people walks through the town at midnight swinging heavy flaming balls of tar, paper, twigs and the like on a rope or chain. Any that survive at the end of the march are thrown into the harbour. If you like the sound of it, you'd better get there before the Health and Safety people stick their oar in.

In the winding streets of **Kirkwall** on the Orkney Islands on New Year's Day they play the *Kirkwall Ba'*, an extraordinary form of football involving most of the men in the town. Players have to try to get the ball from the centre of the town to either end, depending on which side they're playing for. Players stick to the teams their fathers and grandfathers played for. As they frequently have no idea where the ball is, the chaotic contest can last from five to eight hours and is like a rugby match crossed with the running of the bulls in Pamplona.

In **Spain** twelve grapes are eaten at midnight on New Year's Eve to ensure twelve happy months ahead. The **Swiss** think the same can result from dripping cream onto the floor (although, being Swiss, they probably clean it up again immediately).

In **Puerto Rico**, children throw buckets of water out of the window at midnight to rid their homes of evil spirits. In **Greece**, St Basil places presents in children's shoes.

Belgian farmers wish their own livestock a Happy New Year. **Romanians** also talk to farm animals on New Year's Day. As it's thought to be bad luck if the creatures talk back, presumably they usually feel pretty lucky.

And a Sarbatori Vesele to you, mate

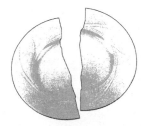

The **Dutch** burn their Christmas trees on bonfires, while in **Ecuador**, a dummy stuffed with newspapers and fireworks is placed outside the home, and is burnt at midnight. The **Danes** throw broken dishes onto each other's front doorsteps; a great many broken dishes means you have a great many friends. Either that, or very rowdy neighbours.

At 11:59 **Americans** watch an illuminated ball, six feet across, take one minute to descend a pole in Times Square. The tradition started in 1907, and the ball was then made of iron and steel; today it's made of Waterford crystal. Light Emitting Diodes (LEDs) will supplement the existing incandescent bulbs for the first time in 2006/7; by 2007/8, the ball will be lit entirely by LEDs.

Hindus in **India** celebrate New Year four times each year – once for each of the four seasons. Parades are big at New Year: in **Nepal** they last four days. In **Oberammergau**, Germany, the parade leader carries a star on a pole and sings about the year that's just ended. In **California**, the Tournament of Roses parade precedes the annual New Year's Day football game.

New Year, rather than Christmas, is the big family-orientated holiday in **Japan**. In December, *Bonenkai* or 'Forget the Year' parties are held to sweep away the problems of the previous year and prepare for the next. Buddhist temples ring their bells 108 times to chase away 108 kinds of human weakness. The festivities end with bulk deliveries of New Year's cars on January 1st.

The biggest New Year's Eve celebrations in the world are in **Rio de Janeiro**, where crowds of over two million people meet on Copacabana beach.

New Year's Eve drinking games

Drinking games are juvenile and silly and we don't approve of them. Any self-respecting adult surely knows that the only real winner will be Captain Hangover and his humungous hammering hammers.

However, forewarned is forearmed. If there is even the remotest possibility that, under the influence of the demon drink, you could be tempted by a less mature friend to put a toe on that oh-so-slippery slope, you should – for reasons of self-preservation – at least know how to play a few.

Here's to the elf of Cardinal Puff

Cardinal Puff

Fans of *Dad's Army* will recall how, in the episode *Fallen Idol*, poor Captain Mainwaring was inveigled into playing this game in the Officer's Mess. It follows a set script which gives the novice little chance of getting through unscathed. There are many versions, but this is the one that so heavily defeated poor Mainwaring.

A drink is placed in front of the player who says the following, with actions.

"Here's to the health of Cardinal Puff for the first time." *(Tap the table with the first finger of your right hand once, tap the table with the first finger of your left hand once. Stamp once with your right foot and once with your left foot. Bang your glass on the table once and take one sip.)*

"Here's to the health of Cardinal Puff Puff for the second time." *(Tap the table with the first and second fingers of your right hand twice, tap the table with the first and second fingers of your left hand twice. Stamp twice with your right foot and twice with your left foot. Bang your glass on the table twice and take two sips.)*

"Here's to the health of Cardinal Puff Puff Puff for the third time." *(Tap the table with the first, second and third fingers of your right hand thrice, and with the first, second and third fingers of your left hand thrice. Stamp thrice with your right foot and thrice with your left foot. Bang your glass on the table thrice and take three sips.)*

Any mistakes and the player should drain the glass and begin all over again. If you are ever persuaded to play, try not to be the first player – unless you've put some serious practice in beforehand. Far better to follow the leader!

Fizzbuzz

Although we first encountered Fizzbuzz as a student drinking game (not that we participated of course), it's also an excellent game to play with kids, as it's a splendid mental arithmetic exercise.

Play goes around in a circle with each player adding one to the previous number, the catch being that if the number is divisible by three, the player should say "Fizz" and if divisible by five, they should say "Buzz". Any number divisible by both three *and* five should be replaced with "Fizzbuzz".

Providing there are no mistakes, the count should go: 1, 2, Fizz, 4, Buzz, Fizz, 7, 8, Fizz, Buzz, 11, Fizz, 13, 14, FizzBuzz, and so on. If there are mistakes, the count should return to zero.

Even when all the players are sober it can be quite tricky and it gets trickier still in some of the game's variants, the most amusing of which have players nod instead of saying the ordinary numbers, only saying out loud "Fizz" and "Buzz". Try replacing even those with noises like blowing raspberries and popping your cheek with your finger and the game becomes wonderfully surreal.

Poo Bum Willy

This is the first cousin to Fizzbuzz in that the players have to count upwards in Roman numerals. Not very exciting in itself except that for the I's they must substitute "poo", for the V's they have to say "bum" and for the X's they must come out with a "willy". Thus what was "I, II, III, IV, V, VI, VII, VIII, IX, X, XI, XII" becomes "Poo, Poo poo, Poo poo poo, Poo bum, Bum, Bum poo, Bum poo poo, Bum poo poo poo, Poo willy, Willy, Willy poo, Willy poo poo", and so on.

It's an incredibly childish game which means it's ideal not only for playing with children who think it's funny to say rude words, but also students and immature adults who think it's amusing having to have a drink every time they get it wrong. That's certainly how we first came across it. Oops! Not a game to play with your Aunt Emily – but then, we don't know your Aunt Emily as well as you do.

What happens when you get to forty? Don't know. Never got that far for shome reashon.

Snapdragon

You may think you like a traditional Christmas, but would you really want to play Snapdragon? Also known as Flapdragon, it was a popular parlour game from the 16th to 19th century, often played on New Year's Eve.

Into a warmed bowl containing a dozen or so raisins you pour brandy that has been heated in a ladle. With the lights off, the brandy is then lit and each player in turn must pluck out a raisin – blue flames dancing about it – and eat it. Although it's possible to singe fingers or the mouth, the temperature of the raisins is much less than you'd expect and, in the dark, there's an extraordinary beauty to the blue flames as the raisin disappears between someone's lips, perhaps why the game has the word 'dragon' in the title.

Other things can be used, such as almonds, grapes or figs; and cognac or even Sambuca can be substituted for the brandy. It's a good idea not to put the bowl on a flammable tablecloth and to keep your table well protected as the flaming brandy can drip all over the place.

Michael Faraday, the 19th-century scientist famed for his work on magnetism and electricity, surmised that the raisins act like miniature wicks. In the same way that brandy poured over Christmas pudding is lit but doesn't damage the pudding, so the temperature isn't high enough to do much damage to people foolish enough to play Snapdragon. Faraday proclaimed that he did "not know a more beautiful illustration of the philosophy of flame". Indeed, unlike the flame of a burning candle, lit alcohol burns with a much cooler, bluer flame but you can reduce the effect on your fingers even further by licking them first.

Flapdragon is mentioned in Shakespeare, both in *Love's Labour Lost* and *Henry IV Part 2*, though it was more of a drinking game than a parlour game back then. It also crops up in Lewis Carroll's *Through the Looking Glass*, when Alice encounters the Snap-dragon-fly with a body made of plum pudding, wings of holly leaves and its head a raisin burning in brandy. It apparently lives on frumenty and mince pie and makes its nest in a Christmas box.

In Robert Chambers' *Book of Days*, published in 1879, the Christmas sport of Snapdragon was said to be accompanied by the following chant:

Here he comes with flaming bowl,
Don't he mean to take his toll,
    Snip! Snap! Dragon!

Take care you don't take too much,
Be not greedy in your clutch,
    Snip! Snap! Dragon!

With his blue and lapping tongue
Many of you will be stung,
    Snip! Snap! Dragon!

For he snaps at all that comes
Snatching at his feast of plums,
    Snip! Snap! Dragon!

But Old Christmas makes him come,
Though he looks so fee! fa! fum!
    Snip! Snap! Dragon!

Don't 'ee fear him, be but bold –
Out he goes, his flames are cold,
    Snip! Snap! Dragon!

The bag game

Each player puts a paper bag on their head, except for the leader (who will be the only one who knows how the game works). The leader then tells everyone to take off something they don't need.

Most people will first remove a shoe, or a watch; the leader describes all the removed items, then instructs everyone to take off something else they don't need.

Eventually, the players will realise that the one thing they don't need is the bag on their head – and they'll take it off, at which point they can stop playing and watch everyone else's discomfort. It's up to the leader to decide how far to go!

If you can't find large enough paper bags, use pillow cases instead. *Don't* be tempted to use plastic carrier bags, even (or especially) if you have been playing drinking games.

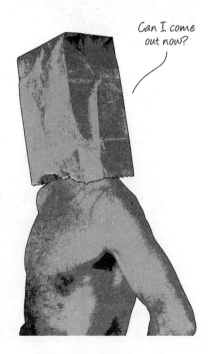

Can I come out now?

Auld Lang Syne

Every New Year's Eve it's the same. The moment the chimes of Big Ben are heard, everyone crosses arms and starts singing Auld Lang Syne, quickly remembering that they know hardly any of the words. They soon find themselves repeating themselves endlessly, perhaps putting in phrases like "for the sake of auld lang syne" that aren't even in there. If only they'd kept their first New Year's resolution of the previous year and learnt the words.

Robert Burns said he'd taken the words down from "an old man's singing", but it's thought he tinkered with it considerably. The original melody has long been lost, the modern tune deriving from a 17th-century Strathspey reel, *The Miller's Wedding* (sometimes known as *The Miller's Daughter*). It's only the first and last verses that are usually sung.

Although it was often sung at the turn of the year towards the end of the 19th century, *Auld Lang Syne* got a real boost in popularity from the Canadian

bandleader Guy Lombardo, who made it an annual feature of his New Year's party broadcast from New York from 1929 onwards.

'Syne' should apparently not be pronounced 'zyne' but 'sign', while 'auld' should rhyme with 'bald'. There was much comment at the New Year's Eve 1999 celebrations in the Millennium Dome when, unlike Tony Blair, the Queen didn't cross her arms while singing it. She, of course, spends rather more time in Scotland than Mr Blair and knew that in Scotland it is customary to cross arms on singing "there's a hand my trusty fiere! And gie's a hand o' thine!" Few non-Scots get that far, of course.

In Japan, the song is known as *Hotaru no hikari* (Glow of a firefly) and is played by many stores to indicate closing time.

Should auld acquaintance be forgot,
And never brought to mind?
Should auld acquaintance be forgot,
And auld lang syne?

For auld lang syne, my dear
For auld lang syne,
We'll tak a cup o' kindness yet,
For auld lang syne!

And surely ye'll be your pint-stowp,
And surely I'll be mine,
And we'll tak a cup o' kindness yet,
For auld lang syne!

For auld lang syne…

We twa hae run about the braes,
And pou'd the gowans fine,
But we've wander'd monie a weary fit,
Sin auld lang syne.

For auld lang syne…

We twa hae paidi'd in the burn
Frae morning sun till dine,
But seas between us braid hae roar'd
Sin auld lang syne.

For auld lang syne…

And there's a hand my trusty fiere,
And gie's a hand o' thine,
And we'll take a right guid-willie waught,
For auld lang syne.

Auld lang syne: old long since, i.e. the days long ago
Pint-stowp: pint tankard
pou'd the gowans: pulled the daisies
fit: footstep
braid: broad
fiere: friend
right guid-willie waught: drink of good fellowship

New Year's resolutions

Probably the only safe resolution is to resolve not to make any resolutions. But you know how it is. A week or more of living it up has taken its toll. You feel bloated, you feel hungover and you may even feel a little guilty at enjoying yourself so unashamedly.

So you determine to give up drinking or to exercise more or to go on a diet. You intend keeping to it, really you do. But have you got what it takes? A quarter of all resolutions we make don't even last until the end of the first week.

Unless you have a will of iron (and you probably wouldn't have overindulged in the first place if you did), then there's only one sensible way to make a New Year's resolution. Announce it. Tell your family or your colleagues what you have resolved to do. With luck, the fear of the inevitable taunts and jeers that will greet your capitulation will keep you on track. Who knows? You might even make it into that second week this year.

Here are some suggestions:

Make a resolution you can keep. The 18th-century British cutter *HMS Resolution* is available from Corel as a beautiful wooden model in 1:50 scale.

Cut your spending on alcohol. As fewer people drink booze in January, you should be able to barter for the price of drinks in bars and restaurants.

Improve your self-image. If you feel overweight, unhealthy and stupid when you're with your friends – change your friends for some who are more overweight, unhealthy and stupid than you are.

Exercise regularly without joining a gym. Buses provide exercise bars and straps which will not only keep you trim, but entertain the other passengers.

Turn over a new leaf every day. To do this you need a book with 730 pages (that's 365 sheets of paper). We can recommend *The Oxford Anthology of English Literature, Volume 7* (OUP, 1973); *Probability and Statistics for Engineers and Scientists* (Prentice Hall, 2001); *Convex Optimization* (CUP, 2004); and the *Euclid 5 Tractor Service Manual* (Euclid, 1958).

9 Christmas recipes

SOME WILL TELL YOU that the real meaning of Christmas is to celebrate the birth of Jesus Christ. Others will say that Christmas is all about gathering your loved ones close to you. In truth, of course, Christmas is really about overindulging to a ridiculous degree, stuffing yourself with good food until you can barely move.

We wouldn't presume to tell you how to cook a turkey but we do have some ideas for what to do with what's left over if the vultures don't strip the bird clean on their first attempt. While we wouldn't snub anyone who buys their Christmas puddings, mince pies or stuffing, those who prefer to give Christmas the home-made touch will find suitably complicated recipes here.

We've a few suggestions for conjuring up nibbles to keep the gannets going between the main bouts and we'll even show you how to get chestnuts roasting on an open fire.

Spending time with children is one of the joys of Christmas, so we're told – as long as they don't come into the kitchen while you're whipping up your masterpiece. We've included a few recipes specially designed for you to make with your brood so they'll feel part of the creative culinary experience.

Hot American turkey salad

One of the best recipes we know for using up leftover turkey, this is a delicious and easy dish that turns cold turkey into something quite special. Even Dad can make this one, so it's perfect for Boxing Day! This recipe serves four, so increase the quantities if you have more turkey.

INGREDIENTS

340g cooked turkey	*2 tsp lemon juice*
4 sticks of celery	*salt and pepper*
4 spring onions	*100g grated Cheddar cheese*
250ml of mayonnaise	*1 packet ready salted crisps*

Chop the turkey into small chunks, and finely slice the celery and spring onions. Mix all the ingredients in a bowl with 80g of the cheese. Turn into a shallow ovenproof dish. Top with the remaining cheese; crumble the crisps and sprinkle them on top. If you have some, sprinkle a little paprika on top for visual interest.

Place in a pre-heated oven at 220°C, 425°F, gas mark 7 for about 10–15 minutes. Don't overcook, or the cheese and mayonnaise sauce will curdle. Serve straight away. ADAPTED FROM *THE AGA BOOK* BY MARY BERRY

Funky turkey sandwich

You had the big blowout hours ago, and everyone's starting to feel a little peckish. Here's a great way to liven up turkey sandwiches to make them a real treat.

INGREDIENTS

1 packet ready salted crisps	*mayonnaise*
handful of cooked turkey	*Pepper*
cranberry sauce	*2 slices bread*

Crush the crisps into small pieces – this is easiest done when they're still in the packet. Combine all the ingredients between two thick slices of fresh bread. Serve to gasps of delight!

Leftover sandwich spread

A good way of using up any cooked meats you have lying around. This one works with just about anything!

INGREDIENTS

cooked meat
1 onion
1 red pepper

2 hard-boiled eggs
mayonnaise
salt and pepper

Dice the meat – using a food processer if you like, but don't turn it into a paste. Dice the onion, pepper, hard-boiled eggs, and mix them with the mayonnaise and seasoning to achieve a thick consistency. Simple, but effective.

Turkey bone soup

After you've used up all your leftover turkey, you'll find yourself with a skeleton on your hands. Not a clean, anatomical skeleton, but one that looks like an extra from *Turkey Zombies of the Evil Dead*, with bits of flesh hanging off it in a gruesome way. Don't throw it away! You can get one more meal out of that obliging bird.

INGREDIENTS

1 large onion, chopped
Cooked turkey carcase
Celery, cabbage, spinach,
or any cooked vegetable

400g white rice
1 chicken stock cube
450g green beans

Fry the onion in a large saucepan, then add the whole turkey carcase. Chop the celery, cabbage and spinach, and add to the pot. Or you could simply add any cooked vegetables left over from Christmas lunch. Pour in enough water to cover, add the rice, and sprinkle the stock cube on the top.

Bring the mixture to the boil, then reduce the heat and simmer for an hour or two, adding more water if it looks like too much is boiling off. At the end, remove the turkey bones as well as any bits of cartilage, skin, parson's nose and other readily identifiable pieces of anatomy. Add the beans, and simmer for 10 minutes.

If you make too much of this, freeze it in small quantities then simply microwave when you want it. That way, you can make Christmas lunch last until Easter!

Smoked salmon profiteroles

Fabulously tasty, and very impressive starters, these are also great finger food
that can be munched with drinks mid morning. Or at any time, really!

INGREDIENTS

50g butter	*1 tbsp lemon juice*
150ml water	*2 tbsp fresh dill*
65g plain flour	*1 tsp horseradish sauce*
2 eggs	*salt and freshly ground pepper*
200g cream cheese	*120g smoked salmon*

Melt the butter in a saucepan, add the water and bring to the boil. Beat in the flour
briskly until the mixture comes away from the side of the pan; allow the mixture to
cool slightly and then gradually beat in the eggs.

Place in a piping bag, and pipe small mounds (the size of a walnut) onto a
dampened baking tray. Bake in a pre-heated oven at 220°C, 425°F, gas mark 7 for
10 minutes. Reduce to 190°C, 375°F, gas mark 5 for a further 10 minutes. Make
a slit in the side of each bun to allow the steam to escape, and cool on a wire rack.

To make the filling, mix the cream cheese, lemon juice, dill, horseradish and
seasoning in a bowl. Spoon the mixture into the choux bun shells, with a folded
slice of smoked salmon on top.

Onion tarts

*It was either
this or come as
a vicar*

Onions work particularly well in this recipe,
although you could use other fillings instead
– see the list at the end.

INGREDIENTS

200g short crust or puff pastry,	*6 medium to large onions,*
as preferred	*thinly sliced into rings*
90g butter	*salt and pepper*

Pre-bake roughly 18 – 20 tartlets at 190°C, 375°F, gas mark 5 for 10 to 15 minutes.
Melt the butter in a thick-bottomed saucepan, and add the onions. Cook on a
medium heat, stirring regularly until they begin to change colour.

Turn the heat down low and stew for 30–45 minutes, stirring regularly until the onions are nicely browned and caramelised. Share the onions between the tartlets and warm in the oven at 190°C, 375°F, gas mark 5 for 10 minutes before serving.

Alternative fillings: pesto and sliced tomatoes (with optional sun-dried tomatoes); sautéed fresh and dried wild mushrooms (preferably ceps) with crème fraiche; stewed aubergine and onion (stew the aubergine for a good 45 minutes); stewed tomato and roasted red pepper (grill or roast the peppers fiercely until blackened to remove the skin before stewing).

Gravad lax

You can buy this from delicatessens, but the stuff you make yourself is much tastier. You do need to think about this one at least week before Christmas!

INGREDIENTS

700g salmon tailpiece, in two fillets
Marinade:
1 tbsp granulated sugar
1 heaped tbsp sea salt
1 tbsp fresh dill (dried would do)
1 tsp crushed black peppercorns
1 tbsp brandy

Sauce:
2 tbsp French mustard
1 tbsp granulated sugar
1 egg yolk
7 tbsp olive oil
2 tbsp wine vinegar
1 rounded tbsp dill
salt and pepper

Mix all the marinade ingredients together and spread on both sides of each piece of salmon, rubbing well into the skin. Then sandwich the fillets together (skin side out) and place in a flat dish with any spare mixture. Cover with foil and weigh down with heavy tins.

Refrigerate for four days, turning each day and rubbing in any spare marinade. Before serving slice the salmon perpendicular to the skin to make chunky rectangular slices.

To make the sauce, beat the mustard with the sugar and egg yolk until smooth. Gradually add the oil and vinegar, beating thoroughly throughout. Season with dill, salt and pepper.

THE RECIPES ON THESE PAGES WERE DEVISED FOR US BY CATHERINE GALLIMORE

Nora's Christmas Pudding

It's okay to buy your Christmas pudding. There are some great ones out there, but there are also plenty of tasteless, dry, dire, almost indigestible puddings that could ruin an otherwise lovely Christmas meal. Luckily you don't have to sit your family down in October or November and get them to test half a dozen because virtually every newspaper – desperate for Christmas copy — will do it for you. Often it's the supermarket premium puds that win out over far more expensive 'luxury' ones.

How much more satisfying to make your own. The sheer time and effort involved greatly increases the eventual pleasure, particularly if you get the kids to help. This recipe for a truly sumptuous pud comes from our friend Carey and has been in her family for 70 years, originating with her gran's cook Nora.

The recipe makes two puddings in two pint basins, each of which will feed 6–8 people with healthy appetites; halve the recipe to make a single pudding.

INGREDIENTS: CHRISTMAS PUDDING

200g shredded suet	100g ground almonds
100g self-raising flour	100g mixed candied peel, finely chopped
breadcrumbs	1 large cooking apple, peeled and finely chopped
cinnamon	grated rind of 1 orange
$\frac{1}{2}$ tsp grated nutmeg	grated rind of 1 lemon
1 tsp mixed spice	4 tbsp brandy
200g soft dark brown sugar	150ml Guinness
200g currants	150ml barley wine
200g sultanas	4 eggs
550g raisins	

In your largest mixing bowl (and it needs to be big), mix the suet and flour thoroughly with a wooden spoon. Add, one by one (mixing each in thoroughly before adding the next) the breadcrumbs, cinnamon, nutmeg, mixed spice, sugar, currants, sultanas, raisins, ground almonds, candied peel, apple, orange and lemon rind. Check carefully as you add each ingredient to make sure you don't miss anything out.

Get another bowl in which to mix the wet ingredients. Put in the brandy, Guinness, barley wine and eggs, and beat with a hand whisk until completely mixed. Pour the wet ingredients into the dry ingredients and stir hard with a wooden spoon. You should expect to need to stir for at least 15 minutes, and maybe more. It is very

I'm sure I left
a sixpence in here
somewhere

hard work, but if everyone has a go – even making a wish as they stir – it can be fun too. The consistency of the mixture will eventually start to change. It will get very sticky and seem to shrink, becoming a little like a very thick liquid. Don't give up. It takes a lot of very tough mixing to get to the required consistency. If you're not sure you're there, keep going. It's not possible to over-mix it.

Cover the bowl with a tea towel and leave it somewhere cool overnight. The following day, grease your pudding basins well (you don't want the puddings to stick on Christmas Day) and fill them with the mixture, packing it in as hard as you can with the back of a wooden spoon. Fill the basins right to the top. Then cover the top of each pudding bowl with a piece of greaseproof paper tied on with cooking string. On top of that, put a muslin square, also tied on with cooking string. Tie the corners of the muslin over the top of the pudding to make a handle.

Steam the puddings for eight hours, watching the water level so that they don't boil dry. When cooked, let them cool, then replace the greaseproof paper and muslin. Store the puddings in a cool place until it's that time of year again. On the big day, steam one or both puddings again for a further two hours. Then loosen the sides with a palate knife and turn the puddings out onto a plate.

Stick some holly in the top, warm some brandy in a ladle then pour over the pudding. Turn the lights off, then light the pudding while everyone applauds.

Serve with lashings of brandy butter.

It is best to make the puddings well in advance. They will keep for a year, but aim to make them by October at the latest. The recipe here is for two puds, so next year's will be ready and waiting for you.

Chestnuts roasting on an open fire

There's nothing like the smell of roasting chestnuts to fill the house with a festive air. Which of us doesn't enjoy roasting our nuts in front of an open fire?

Can I come out now?

Ideally, you'll have a chestnut roaster in which to hold the chestnuts; if you can't find one, a baking tin is a suitable substitute.

Cut a slit in the top of each chestnut to allow the expanding air to escape. If you don't, they're likely to explode – which isn't as much fun as it sounds.

Chestnuts take between 10 and 20 minutes to cook on an open fire, depending on the heat. Give the tin or roaster a shake every couple of minutes, or the chestnuts are in danger of getting burnt on one side.

If you don't have access to a real fire, they can be cooked in the oven. Place in a baking tin and cook at 200°C, 400°F, gas mark 6, for around 30 minutes. For the authentic al fresco experience, serve in small paper bags and charge £2 a time.

The best chestnut stuffing

We've made this every year, and it's a fantastic recipe. It's not hard to do, and is so much better than those cardboard substitutes that come in cardboard packets. Fresh chestnuts are a hassle to cook and prepare; frozen or tinned chestnuts will do just as well.

INGREDIENTS

100g streaky bacon
1 large onion, chopped
450g chestnuts, chopped
2 tbsp freshly chopped parsley

75g fresh brown breadcrumbs
1 egg, beaten
salt and pepper

Fry the bacon until crisp, then remove from the pan and keep to one side. Add the chopped onion to the fat in the pan, fry until almost soft then add the chestnuts. Cook for five more minutes. Remove from the heat, add the bacon, parsely and breadcrumbs, and bind together with the egg; add salt and pepper to taste. Stuff inside the body of your turkey before cooking.

ADAPTED FROM *THE AGA BOOK* BY MARY BERRY

Who works at MI6 at Christmas?

Mince Spies!

Mince pies

Even if you buy delicious mince pies, you're unlikely to be complimented on your fantastic shopping skills. Far better to make your own. This glorious – and slightly boozy – mincemeat recipe has travelled 9,000 miles from our chum Judith's mum in Perth, Australia. Ideally, you should give the mixture six weeks' head start on Christmas to let the flavours develop.

INGREDIENTS

350g raisins
225g sultanas
225g currants
100g mixed peel
225g glacé cherries, red and green
100g chopped peanuts (or almonds)
450g apples
350g dark brown sugar
½ cup of brandy

grated rind of 1 orange, 1 lemon
juice of 1 lemon
2 tsp mixed spice
½ tsp grated nutmeg
150g butter
short crust or puff pastry
milk for glazing
icing sugar

Chop up the raisins, sultanas, currants and mixed peel. Add the cherries, chopped in half (mostly red, some green for aesthetics), and the chopped peanuts (or blanched almonds).

Peel, core and grate the apples and add them with all their juice. Add the sugar, the lemon and orange rind, lemon juice, mixed spice, nutmeg and melted butter. Add more exotic fruit like dried pineapple or mango if you fancy. Finally, pour in a generous slug of brandy.

Cover and place the mixture in the fridge. Stir it every other day. After a few days, you might feel the need to add a little brandy. (This is our sort of recipe.) It needs to be moist but not gloopy.

Whether using bought pastry (short crust or puff is good) or your own, roll it thinly. Mince pies should major on the contents, not the shell. Form around dollops of the mixture in a baking tin; cover with pastry, and brush with milk. Place in the oven at 220°C, 425°F, gas mark 7 for about 15 minutes. Shake icing sugar over them when they've cooled.

If I wasn't elf-employed I'd ask for an increase in celery

Avocado dip

If you want to conjure up a simple but delicious dip, this should do the trick.
It tastes as good as guacamole but involves far less hassle.

INGREDIENTS

ripe avocado
1 tbsp soured cream or crème fraiche
1 tbsp mayonnaise

Lemon juice
celery, carrot, cucumber etc to serve

Take a ripe avocado (squishy but not brown is what you're after), halve it and
scoop the insides out and into a blender. Add the soured cream, mayonnaise and a
dash or two of lemon juice, then blend until you've got a smooth paste. Until you're
confident, put in less than you need of the juice, mayonnaise and sour cream and
keep tasting and adding until you've got it right.

Serve it in a bowl, nicely arranging sliced carrot, cucumber, celery or whatever
you prefer around it. Pringles or Kettle chips will do fine if you haven't got anything
healthier left in the house.

If you're not serving it straight away, cover it with clingfilm, ensuring that it's
actually touching the surface of the dip, otherwise it will turn an unappetising
shade of brown. Leaving the avocado stone in the dip is also supposed to help
it stay fresh – well, it works when the avocado's still on the tree, after all. If you
forget, stirring the dip will probably be enough to restore a green hue.

Incidentally, the word 'avocado' is derived from the Aztec word for testicle, which
apparently they thought it resembled. You probably didn't want to know that.

Christmas cake with brandy

Here's one that's as much fun to make as it is to eat.

INGREDIENTS

One bottle of brandy	*Half a dozen eggs*
Loads of mixed fruit, raisins and stuff	*Sugar, maybe some flour too*
Don't forget the butter	*Did we mention the brandy?*

Assemble all the ingredients. If the brandy has been opened, taste it to ascertain that it hasn't been watered down. If still sealed, open and taste to check it hasn't gone off. Put raisins, sultanas, mixed peel and dry fruit into a bowl or saucepan.

Add a cup of brandy. Have one for yourself while you're at it. Blend the fruit mixture with a processor. Add in the butter and two eggs and mix with a spoon until your arm hurts. Have a cup of brandy to revitalise yourself halfway through, then have another go.

Put in half of the sugar, sugar, honey, baby love, then pour in a bit more sugar, sugar, candy girl. If you're pouring one anyway, I don't mind if I do.

Get the other four eggs and juggle with them. Oops. Three eggs, then. Oops. Clear that up later. A quick brot of shandy to keep out the cold. Turn on the processor and vary the speed as you go round the track at Silverstone, vroom, vroom, out of Brooklands and into Priory. Shhhhhhh! Mustn't wake the kids.

Jusht another lickle shlurp

Add a table of sugar. No sugar. Salt will do, then cry another tup. Then get on the table with a spoon. Grease something or other while the oven gets turned on. Put the bowl upside down on your head while you're waiting.

Best not leave the brandy out in case the cat gets its tongue caught in it. Just time for a quick nightcup. Well, all right, just the one. Then I'm going to bed.

Cooking with kids

You really *don't* want kids in the kitchen on Christmas day. But if you've an hour or so to spare in the days either side, here are a few great ways they can take part with the minimum amount of stress.

Angel biscuits

Entertaining to serve, and fun to make. This recipe makes around 12 cookies.

INGREDIENTS

180g butter	*180g plain flour*
125g caster sugar	*To decorate the biscuits: Smarties,*
1 egg	*silver ball cake decorations*
70g self-raising flour	*200g milk cooking chocolate*

Pre-heat the oven to 180°C, 350°F, gas mark 4. Place the butter and sugar into the bowl of an electric mixer and beat until light, whipped and creamy.

Add the egg and beat well. Stir in both flours and mix to a dough. Roll out the dough and create angel shapes with wings, a body and a head.

Line a baking tray with non-stick baking paper. Place the dough angels onto the tray. Press your thumb into the middle of each biscuit being careful not to press through to the tray (this is a knack, go gently at first). Fill each hole with two or three differently coloured Smarties. Bake for 10–12 minutes or until cookies are golden. Cool on wire racks. To decorate, first melt the chocolate according to the packet instructions. Cover the head and wingtips with warm chocolate. Before the chocolate sets, add two Smarties for eyes and a row of silver balls for the hair and mouth (only bigger children can do this neatly, so tell the small ones it doesn't matter if the angels' faces aren't perfect).

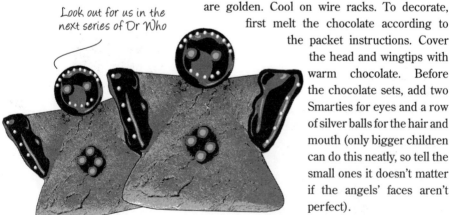

Look out for us in the next series of Dr Who

Edible snowflakes

No doubt at some point your kids will bring home paper snowflakes that they've made at school. It's probably in the curriculum. There may even be a GCSE in it.

Chances are they haven't made edible snowflakes, though. Get some flour tortillas and fold them in half and then in half again, being careful not to press too hard or they'll tear. When folded, snip some bits out just as you would with paper snowflakes. They'll look even better if you fold them into six (first fold in half, then do a double-fold inwards), but it's harder to manage with tortillas than paper.

Opened out, you *should* now have something resembling a snowflake. Ignore the instructions on the packet to heat in the microwave or oven. Instead, heat some oil in a pan and fry each until it's crisp.

You can then sprinkle them with icing sugar, or butter them. You could even put cinammon and sugar on, jam, honey or indeed anything your kids fancy.

Edible snowmen

Marshmallow popcorn balls may not be the healthiest food you can give your kids but they're pretty yummy. Make up a 100g microwaveable pack of popcorn. Put it in a greased baking tray and keep it warm in the oven.

Melt 75g or so of butter in a saucepan on a lowish heat then stir in a 250g pack of white mini marshmallows. Keep stirring until it's all melted then pour it over the popcorn and mix it all up well.

With a little butter or vegetable oil on your hands to stop the stuff sticking, form the gloop into spheres about the size of cricket balls. Make them into miniature snowmen by fixing one ball atop a slightly larger ball with a flat bottom so it will stand up. Use assorted sweets for the coat buttons, eyes, nose and mouth, strawberry bootlaces for a scarf, and Twiglets for arms.